Still Here!

Still Here!

BOBBY GEORGE

The King of Bling

With Dave Bracegirdle

pitch

First published by Pitch Publishing, 2025

Pitch Publishing
9 Donnington Park,
85 Birdham Road,
Chichester, West Sussex,
PO20 7AJ
www.pitchpublishing.co.uk
info@pitchpublishing.co.uk

A CIP catalogue record is available for this book from the British Library.

ISBN 978 1 83680 159 7

FSC www.fsc.org MIX Paper | Supporting responsible forestry FSC® C010615

Printed and bound on FSC® certified paper in line with our continuing commitment to ethical business practices, sustainability and the environment.

Printed and bound in India by Thomson Press

CONTENTS

I dedicate this book to Harry Kicks (junior), my great friend and partner in crime.

INTRODUCTION

'THAT'S THE last book gone, Bobby,' said one of the hard-working assistants manning the merchandising stall. It was the summer of 2023 and I was covering one of the World Seniors Darts events for television.

It wasn't just the final book on the stall: the very last copy of my autobiography had finally been sold; the story of the first 50-odd years of my life was all gone, no longer available to buy.

Initially, I thought no more of it. I had never really intended to do that book in the first place but so much had been crammed into my life by then that the constant demands to put it all in print finally wore me down and I was happy to go along with it.

As many of you will know, I ended up having a successful career as a professional darts player but it was something that I stumbled into; never having thrown a dart until I was 30. Over the next decade I won some of the biggest prizes going and travelled the world alongside the biggest characters in the game. My story became theirs and vice versa; so much was shared, so many high jinks and escapades.

Throughout my years on the oche I developed a loyal fanbase who were always there for me, cheering from the rafters when I won and helping to pick me up during the darker times. Thankfully, many of them keep in touch and come and say hello when they see me out and about or at the big darts events. I'm genuinely fortunate that so many care and ask after me. 'Still here,' I tell them – and I'm glad that they're 'still here' as well.

Since the last book, I've done so many things; appearing on virtually every daytime and celebrity television programme as well as playing bit parts in several Hollywood movies. My big screen credits now involve doing a movie with Johnny Depp, no less. Whilst we got on like a house on fire I think it's probably fair to say that my wife Marie was a little more excited about meeting the great man than I was!

As good as those things have been, I'm probably best known these days as one of the 'national treasures' (their words, not mine!) from the factual documentary series *The Real Marigold Hotel* and *Gone To Pot: American Road Trip*. Those programmes have taken me to parts of the world that I never thought I'd see and given me that many amazing adventures that I decided it might be an idea to share them with you.

So, the idea of *Still Here* was born; a look at many of the things I've done over the past 20 years, whilst also taking the time to give a refresher on some of the key moments from earlier in my life.

There's the harrowing account of how a ruptured spleen nearly killed me and a reminder of how I broke my back on stage and spent part of my recovery time building George Hall, our dream home.

Oh – and I know it's careless of me – but I've lost a few toes along the way as well. If you're the squeamish type you might want to miss that bit!

May the darts be with you,

Bobby

Ardleigh, Essex

ICE CREAM BOBBY?

I'VE ALWAYS loved ice cream. Who doesn't? I've never really been keen on too many fancy desserts or puddings but offer me a bit of ice cream to round off a nice meal and I'm a happy old soul.

I'm sure the medics would say it's not that good for you but it's never done me any harm. Or hadn't, until I went on a television programme a few years ago. You may have seen it – *Gone To Pot: American Road Trip*. The clue was in the title really.

Having already done some television documentaries on how you can improve your life as a senior citizen, I thought this was going to be something similar when I got a phone call from Ros Edwards, a television talent producer, asking if I'd be interested in going to America for a few weeks to feature in a fact-finding show they were making for ITV.

'What's it all about?' I asked naively.

They told me it was about exploring the medical benefits of taking marijuana. In certain states in the USA it's legal to buy the stuff and for many people it has been proven to provide pain relief, control inflammation and help with all sorts of ailments from dementia to cancer, arthritis to rheumatism and other general pains.

I wasn't into any hippy stuff back in my younger days. Working hard for a living, playing darts and enjoying a few beers was my lot. I certainly had never been interested in taking drugs. This was different, and I was intrigued to find out if it could do me any good, as I've lived in almost constant pain for much of the last 30 years. Those that have followed my darting career or read my first book *Bobby Dazzler, My Story* may know that I sustained a freak injury on stage, playing in the 1994 World Championships at the Lakeside Country Club in Frimley Green.

During my quarter-final match against Liverpool's Kevin Kenny I celebrated the winning of a leg by getting a little too excited. I leapt in the air and let out a celebratory roar, 'Yes, c'mon Bo.' [I've always called myself 'Bo' and Eric Bristow used to call me that as well.] As I landed, I felt a sharp pain in my back. Subsequently, having played my semi-final and final in absolute agony it transpired that I'd broken my back.

I was fortunate not to have been paralysed but I still required immediate surgery, which my £16,000 runners-up cheque helped to finance. Eight titanium screws, each around two inches long, were inserted into the base of my spine to help me on to the long road to recovery.

It's given me plenty of gip ever since and like a lot of people my age I'd love to roll back the years and wake up pain-free each day. I'd never taken marijuana before but had an open mind about it. Some say it's good, some bad but I felt I'd like to find out for myself. Wasn't it John Lennon who said, 'Don't knock it until you've tried it'?

There are more and more states in America that are making it legal to use marijuana and whilst it's still outlawed over here, there's a growing feeling that those in need of pain relief should be able to access it.

Does it do any good? Well, that's what we were supposedly sent to try to find out.

Meeting up in San Francisco, I discovered my fellow travellers to be stars of stage and screen Linda Robson, Pam St Clement and Christopher Biggins, plus former footballer John Fashanu. I'd met Biggins and Linda before but didn't know Pam or John at all. Understandably, whilst breaking the ice with a couple of drinks after our long flight, the conversation quickly turned towards the reason for our trip.

At the start of the documentary we were described as 'five national treasures' but as we set out on our adventure we felt more like five gullible guinea pigs.

I sensed early on that four of us were very open-minded about trying the stuff for ourselves, whilst John was far more reticent. Ideally, I suppose, for a programme like that, you need a bit of Yin and Yang, differing views on whether the drug should be made more widely available. But it was pretty clear what we'd signed up for and I struggled to see what John was going to bring to the party with his reluctance.

Even if the marijuana didn't send us nutty as a fruitcake, our psychedelic minibus might do the job anyway. A 21st-century recreation of the Beatles' Magical Mystery Tour bus, it wasn't something you could stare at for too long. We dubbed it the Magical Marijuana Mystery Tour.

It was clear that we needed some instruction on how to get hold of the drug, what to take and in what quantities. Chris, our tour guide and driver, explained the procedure to us and it couldn't have been any easier – maybe too easy, in fact. We went to see a local doctor – at least I assume it was a doctor. For all I know it could have been just a local spiv we were talking to, we honestly wouldn't have known any different.

He asked us about our respective conditions and I told him that I was on 16 tablets a day for pain relief after breaking my back, had shocking arthritis in my hips and had pain in my feet having had four toes removed. (I'll tell you about that later!)

Individually we all met the necessary 'criteria' and for a princely sum of $100 each, we were issued with our prescriptions. It was so easy, it looked like a right con to me but that's what we were there for, so off we went to a dispensary, called The World of Weed, or something like that, to see if there was anything suitable for us to try.

A little bit like entering an airport, we had to take our passports with us and then were screened as we went through, just in case we had inadvertently forgotten to tell them we were carrying any weapons or anything on us.

Once we were in it was like a mini supermarket. The place was rammed full of stuff, all containing cannabis for medicinal purposes. You could buy anything you wanted: soap or cakes or biscuits or chocolate – and do you know, you can even buy fanny cream? Instead of KY Jelly you can use some fanny cream that's got marijuana in it!

Linda, Pam and Biggins each emerged with a bag of goodies and I said I'd try some of theirs but Fash was far more reluctant. I still felt it was wrong to go on a programme like that and condemn something before you know what it does, but he didn't want to know.

In very small quantities the rest of us each tried some of the cake or chocolate but not to the extent we could form any sort of opinion on it.

A day or two later we were taken to a church and I wondered if we were going to see somebody baptised or something, but it was clearly used for other purposes these days. This bloke explained to me that his mate had bought the old church intending to convert it into apartments, but he'd instead been persuaded to leave it as somewhere that people could go in and smoke marijuana. The new owner had, surprisingly, agreed, as long as the community paid the rates and provided funds for any upkeep. So they did: they painted it up and made a very good job of it and made it into a place that served the whole community. There were loads of toys and rides where you could take the kids but there was also a place where you could go and relax and get stoned out of your fucking head if that was your thing.

He asked if I wanted a joint, so I said, 'Yeah, I'll have one with you.'

Fash was quick to jump in and offer his opinion. 'That's disgusting,' he said to me.

I asked him what he meant by that and he told me that I shouldn't be smoking in God's house because this was where people came to pray. He wasn't aware that the church was no longer used for religious purposes, so I told him and added, 'You don't have to come into a building to do that, you can pray to God in your toilet if you want to!'

'Ignore him, he's just a prick,' I said to the old bloke and had a couple of puffs with him, aware that we were becoming more and more exposed to the drug each day.

We were taken to loads of outlets that you could buy these goods from, including a vet's surgery that provided the same sort of stuff for animals. If your cat or dog or budgie or something had an ailment, cancer of the pancreas or skin cancer or whatever, they claimed that this stuff would help cure them.

Take your poorly racehorse down and, Bob's your uncle, give him a 'biscuit' and he'll be cured.

We moved down the coast from San Francisco to Los Angeles and were taken to a club called Puff, Pass and Paint. Admission was $39 for two hours and it was basically a warehouse where you get stoned, under the pretence that you're attending an art class. You all sit around this table and there's something in the middle to draw or paint – with us it was a cactus in a pot. Whilst you're busily being creative, a bong is being passed around the table and you all have a puff. A bong is a glass pipe filled with water. As you inhale, the cannabis smoke is filtered and cooled by the water. There's no smell to it and you don't know you're taking anything but it gets in your head in about four seconds flat and you're suddenly high as a kite.

You're all there doing your painting, la di la, chatting and humming away, then suddenly BANG. You think you're producing a masterpiece and can't see how bad it all is.

When I was young I was quite good at painting and drawing and fancied going to art college but when the subject was raised with my dad all he said was, 'Who do you think you are, Leonardo da Vinci? Get to work!'

It was never mentioned again. Now, thousands of miles away, my talent with a paintbrush resurfaced and my cactus in a pot was acknowledged as the best, although most of us were well out of it by the time they came to judge our efforts.

They'd brought us a couple of little tumblers, one with red wine in and one half-filled with water, to wash our brushes in. I was so bad by the end that I actually got confused and mixed my tumblers up, washing my red paint brush out in the water and then drinking it, instead of the wine!

Pam St Clement loved it and got high as a kite; she got the giggles about it and couldn't stop laughing at me.

One of the cameramen had been filming me and kept egging me on. I asked him if he'd ever tried it and he said he'd briefly had a go in his college days, so I passed him the bong and told him to have a go. I gave him some wine as well and within a minute or two he was helpless and could no longer use the camera because he was giggling along with the rest of us. It was one of the funniest experiences I saw there and I was helplessly crying with laughter. It was a shame they didn't use any footage of that in the series: maybe it was to save our blushes but it would have been hilarious to watch it back.

Friends have asked me what the experience felt like and I can only say that it was all very relaxing, the sort of feeling you get when you've had about four pints of lager.

Maybe you're so relaxed that you can't feel any pain but I sense that it does have some healing properties. I'm sure there are benefits to using it and certainly there are plenty of believers that swear by its usage. One fascinating story I remember from being there was when I was sat chatting to a lady who, like me, was getting on a bit in years. I asked her how long she had been taking the stuff.

'Not long,' she told me, then went on to say that her boys had often used it at home but she couldn't stand the smell so made them smoke it outside.

Then she told me that she'd got breast cancer and they had to remove one of her breasts. So, she went through all that trauma and then had all the treatment afterwards but after a few months it came back again on the other side. They told her to prepare for more surgery but she was adamant that she wasn't going to go through all that again.

'It was hellish and I couldn't face it again,' she told me. 'I couldn't handle it again, so thought if I pass away then I pass away.'

Someone suggested she try a herbal doctor and he put her on the marijuana. Do you know what? It got rid of it. She told me that she had her own little name for marijuana, she called it the Plant of Life. I always remembered her and her little pet name and when I got back home I had some darts shirts made up with marijuana all over them in glitter and on the back it said The Plant of Life. It was just my little tribute to her but when I started wearing the shirts at darts exhibitions I think everyone thought I'd become a pothead. If I went for a quiet drink at the end of an evening I'd get guys sidling up to me at the bar – 'Want a joint, Bob?' – and then pressing one into my hand. Some nights, depending on where I was, there would be the offer of 14 or 15 a night.

I'd always refuse. 'No, no thanks,' I'd say, leaving them feeling very confused I'm sure.

A couple of days after we'd been to Puff, Pass and Paint, we were taken to the house of Nonna Marijuana for an experience I'll never forget. This 94-year-old lady incorporates marijuana into her cooking and we'd been invited around for dinner. She'd made two pans of gnocchi for us to try, one containing a small amount of marijuana butter and one without. Some of the others were keen to sample her added ingredient but I resisted, not being a big fan of gnocchi anyway.

When added to food, it can take up to two hours for marijuana to have any effect and Nonna mentioned that she'd only used a small amount in any case. We were having a nice evening, chatting away normally, and it was perfectly natural for me to accept when offered some ice cream for afters. I didn't know that it contained one of Nonna's special 'kicks', so happily allowed her to fill my bowl, putting five big scoops in. Biggins did the same and even Fash said he'd try a little bit.

It just tasted like vanilla and chocolate and I gobbled it down but by the time we were back on the coach, a couple of hours had passed and I began to feel awful. My head was spinning and I could sense that I was in a bit of trouble. Biggins was worse. He looked like a zombie and couldn't speak. Then it hit me properly. I was sick at the back of the bus and began to cry. Totally disorientated, I'd never experienced anything like it. It felt like being seasick 100 times over and like the worst hangover I'd ever had. I honestly thought I was going to die and don't remember anything else. Both Biggins and I had to be looked after by the production crew; we were in a bad way.

Unbeknown to me at the time, our accommodation for that evening was called the Madonna Inn, which was known for having themed rooms. Mine had a Flintstones-type theme to it, caves and stuff everywhere. So, when I woke up the next morning I didn't have a clue where I was, but just presumed I'd died and gone to heaven – or the other place. Blinking my way back into consciousness, I looked up and saw rocks all over the ceiling.

'Fucking hell, the plastering is a bit rough,' I said, out loud.

'Oh, Bobby's back.'

My head hurt as I moved and looked to my left. It was Linda.

I was struggling to make sense of anything at all but something needed addressing straight away. There was a big double bed. I was there and so was Linda.

'Erm, we didn't, did we?' I stammered.

'No,' she shrieked, 'we didn't!'

Bless her, Linda had been so concerned about my welfare, she was perched on the edge of my bed just making sure I was going to be alright.

Having a few puffs of marijuana can have a gentle side-effect to most people but when it's added to food you have to be extra careful. Very small quantities is the key and I'd learned a very sharp lesson and vowed there and then that I'd never eat it again.

I've not taken anything since but if I ever got to a point where I couldn't walk properly or was in so much pain with my back or from my feet that I felt it would do me some good, I'd happily take it, assuming it was prescribed, of course.

It's not a cure-all and it's not for everyone; it doesn't work for everybody, so it's not down to me to tell anyone to go ahead and take this or that and you'll be cured instantly. But for some people it does seem to have healing benefits.

One thing I would add is that the stuff we saw and were given in America was the proper stuff, nothing dodgy about it at all. It wasn't grown in someone's attic or back garden but grown under government conditions, without any pesticides or insecticides or anything. Produced in mass quantities, it was all grown in giant warehouses, with bright lights and all the proper fans. This stuff was the pure plant, nothing else.

I'm glad I went and did the documentary, even if it put me off ice cream for life – which, thankfully, it didn't.

BACKTRACKING

AT THIS point it might be worth having a refresher, just in case you might be imagining that this is just a résumé of an elderly gentleman's dope-smoking experiences.

For the first 30 years of my life my occupation might have been described as an odd-jobber, or labourer. I became a bloody good industrial granite floor-layer and made a few quid at that game as well. But it wasn't all that I did because I'd learned a lot of crafts from my dear old dad through necessity, as his eyesight packed up on him. I became skilled at all sorts of things as a youngster and it prepared me well, as I set off into the big wide world after leaving school at 14 with no qualifications.

Cycling ten miles to work each day, my first job was at a flower nursery where I helped sow the flowers and bedding plants and then took them to market to sell. My duties would involve a weekly trip to Covent Garden, where all sorts of scams and money-making opportunities would present themselves. Many of those activities were revealed in my first book and whilst one or two stories may be duplicated along the way, we'll leave my journey from schoolboy to scallywag for now.

After about 18 months of working at George Abbott's flower nursery in Romford, my mate Eric Pratt hooked me up with a job at B. Finch Ltd in Barkingside, working on building maintenance. It meant double the money I'd been on at the flower nursery and enabled me to learn some proper trades. In time I was taught the necessary skills in bricklaying, joinery, painting, plastering and plumbing. Unlike school, where nothing seemed to sink in, I found I had an appetite for each of these crafts and really enjoyed broadening my knowledge.

It is amazing to think how invaluable it all became, because around 30 years later I would go on to build my own home, George Hall, near Ardleigh in Essex. In a sense I was the original Bob the Builder!

They taught me so much at Finch's and it was a wrench to leave but just before my 18th birthday I was offered an opportunity to increase my wages by accepting a job to help dig out the new Victoria Line tunnels on the London Underground. This was physically demanding work and I could be shovelling out the earth for up to 16 hours a day; it was a good job that I was a big, strong lad and able to cope. Others weren't so fortunate and didn't last long down there. I did that for about three years, before taking on other jobs, including being a nightclub bouncer, a painter and decorator, a window cleaner and then a granite floor layer.

By the end of the 1960s I was married to Betty and daughter Nicola and son Shane came along soon after. It was a marriage of convenience really and didn't stand a chance of lasting as I worked away from home so often and even when I was there we didn't really have much in common, except the children.

My one passion in life, away from grafting hard to earn a living, was fishing. I'd done it a lot as a young lad and really enjoyed spending a day by a lake or on a riverbank. Opportunities for a bit of fishing once I was working were rare, although I would jump at the chance if it came along.

One day that chance presented itself. Malcolm Ellis, one of the lads from my local boozer, mentioned that he was going sea fishing in Ireland and wondered if I'd be interested in going along with him. We went to a place called Kinsale, 20 miles south of Cork, where our hopes of a peaceful, calm couple of days' fishing were dashed by the choppiest of conditions. Our little boat was going up and down and turning our stomachs inside out. I'd never experienced anything like it before and was a little relieved when Malcolm suggested that we spent the next day in a little pub he'd seen called the Lobster Pot.

Two or three pints in, Malcolm had noticed that a couple of lads fancied themselves on the dartboard and suggested we take them on. I knew he was a keen player but I'd never touched a set in my life and certainly didn't know what you were supposed to hit. Malcolm told me not to worry, he'd let me know what to throw for and for the rest of the afternoon and into the evening we went unbeaten. 'Hit the 20 Bob,' he'd say and I did.

For some reason I seemed to have an aptitude for it. I needed him to tell me where to throw but once I had that information I found it relatively easy to hit the nominated target. I must have made an impression on Malcolm because he kept saying I was a natural and suggested I take darts up seriously. Nothing could have been further from my mind, especially as the weather cleared up in Ireland and we had a great few days of fishing before returning home.

I'd practically forgotten about our exploits on the Lobster Pot's dartboard until one evening in our local, the Old Maypole in Barkingside, when I allowed myself to get talked into a money match against a known gobshite by the name of Kenny the Mouth. He just happened to be the best player in there and played in the same team as Malcolm. I didn't like him and thought he was nothing more than a bully and I don't like bullies!

Accepting his challenge, I beat him fair and square.

Malcolm couldn't stop beaming and reiterated that I ought to consider taking darts a little more seriously. With his encouragement I decided there and then to give it a go and suddenly darts enveloped my whole life. Playing and practising was the only thing that mattered and I began to play league darts every night and enter as many open tournaments as I could.

Every time I stepped up to the oche to play a game I knew I was improving and even though I was still earning a living through laying floors, I managed to find a way to combine my day job with starting to make a name for myself at darts.

I drove an old 1600E Ford Cortina automatic at the time and took out the back seats to get all my shovels in there. On many occasions when I was away from home, either laying floors or playing darts, I'd kip in the back as well. The thing with the floors was that you always had some time to kill whilst the cement dried, so I'd take a dartboard along with me and practise all my finishing combinations.

Most players used a standard set of out-shots to finish a leg but I spent a lot of hours looking at different combinations and discovered you could give yourself a better chance if you incorporated a dart at 25 or bull. At school I'd never been any good at mathematics (or many other subjects for that matter!) but the more I studied the board the more obvious it became. For example, if you left yourself 94, the standard way would be to throw for treble 18 to leave double top. That's fine if your first dart lands, but if it doesn't then you are chasing a different treble or you won't get a throw at a double. My way, I'd back myself on most occasions to hit either a 25 or bull. A 25 would leave me 69 – and a potential 19, bull finish. A bullseye would leave me 44, either a 4 and tops or a 12 and double 16. Give yourself a chance.

It was quite funny to hear some of the commentators once I'd started to appear on television. Several claimed that I'd 'lost count' and didn't know what to throw for. It might have been unorthodox but I knew alright – and was the first to introduce that style of finishing – a style that every top professional now incorporates in their game.

Despite making rapid strides within the sport, I was still out every day laying the floors and making sure that I did a good job for all of my customers. This was my bread and butter; if I played a bad game of darts it didn't matter so much but if I laid a bad floor then I wouldn't get paid.

One day I managed to land myself a nice little contract working on an industrial estate at Aylesbury in Buckinghamshire. Across the road from where I was working was a pub called the John Kennedy. Better than that, it was a darts pub. The landlord was a keen player himself and they ran several teams in the local leagues. Needless to say, I began to go in every lunchtime and play against the regulars, beating them up good and proper. They'd encourage me to stay for as long as I could and then come back in the evenings and play some more.

After a hard day's graft, laying the floor, we had a break to allow everything to settle for a few hours before going back at around 10.30pm to finish the job. This gave me a bit of time to go back to the pub and challenge the locals again. The landlord would test me at first and say, 'Get a 180 and I'll get you a beer on the house.'

Well, it was on an old elm board and I hit so many 180s in the end he said, 'Just help yourself whenever you want a drink.' Some days I was well pissed and staggered my way back to work.

Word soon got about that I was hot on the dartboard and the place would be packed with fellas coming in, trying to beat me. I was clearly good for the takings and the landlord sensed a further opportunity to cash in.

'We've had Leighton Rees in here, playing all night,' he told me. Leighton was already an established star and would go on to become the first British Darts Organisation (BDO) World Champion, winning the inaugural event in 1978. Even before then, he was a major draw wherever he went.

'Alright, was he?' I enquired.

'Yeah, it was a good night,' he said. 'He charged £150, what do you charge?'

'Oh, the same,' I said, thinking on my feet.

'That's alright with me,' said the landlord, before adding, 'When can you do it?'

My immediate thought was that I'd be happy to do it now, straight away, for that sort of money but we sat down and talked sensibly and came up with a date. When it came around I gave them a great night and everyone was really pleased with how it had gone. Word got around quickly and I was suddenly getting as many bookings as I could handle, all for 150 quid a pop. I'd never even contemplated doing it for a living but I suddenly began to see all sorts of prospects opening up for me. Everyone was trying to get hold of me to go and perform at their pub or club. From nowhere, the demand blew up out of all proportion.

Initially I was just so happy that someone had booked me to entertain them that I'd happily play all night, playing against anyone that wanted to face me. It didn't matter if I played ten or 20 opponents, I just wanted to beat them all and usually did. This was long before mobile phones or emails had even been thought of, so everything was done by word of mouth with a lot of good faith on both sides. They trusted that I'd turn up and I trusted that they would pay me!

But, I realised that things needed to be run a little better and was having a good think about how I could go about it. What I really needed was a contract with a brewery.

GAINING COURAGE

THE FISHING trip had been in the autumn of 1976 and things moved quickly from that point onwards as I began to make my mark in the game. I qualified for a couple of high-profile events in my first year, playing in the Winmau World Masters at Wembley and having a run to my first *News of the World* Championship, although that day at the grand finals turned a little sour, as you'll hear later.

I then lifted the North American Open title on my first trip abroad and was rapidly climbing the world rankings, all whilst continuing to put in a hard shift laying floors each day.

Fit and healthy, I was more than content to see where life would take me at that stage, but I was increasingly aware that more possibilities would open up for me if I had more time to concentrate on my darts. Criss-crossing the country for my darts engagements and work commitments made for a tough existence at times and I spent many nights kipping in the back of the car. I remember on a couple of occasions waking up in lay-bys and being in so much of a hurry to get to my next engagement that I even used water from a puddle to have a shave with, so that I would look a little bit more refreshed for my next customer.

Desperate to end what was becoming a frantic cycle, I thought long and hard about what needed to change for me and the answer arrived with the help of a brewery.

One day I was near to London Bridge, working in one of the railway arches laying a floor and had some time to kill whilst it dried. Courage Breweries had one of their main offices nearby and I'd heard mention of a guy who looked after things on their promotional side. 'It can't hurt to see if he can put anything my way,' I thought.

I wasn't exactly dressed for any fancy meetings but it seemed like now was as good a time as any. I'd got concrete on my boots but kicked them against the door outside before I went in.

The foyer was suitably impressive and I had to walk across a large red carpet to get to the reception desk, where a woman did her best to ignore me at first. Standing there, feeling like a wally, I looked around and thought 'Fuckin' hell.' All the way from the door to the desk was a trail of concrete footprints, where I'd walked. 'This is a good start,' I thought.

'Can I help you?'

At last my presence was recognised. 'Hello doll,' I said to her. 'Is your promotions manager in? Can I see him?'

'Have you got an appointment, sir?'

I told her that I knew he worked there and that I had an idea that he may be interested in. She pressed a few numbers on her switchboard and rang him up and after a few seconds I was ushered in.

Dave Clarke was his name and he was clearly surprised to see me and asked what I was doing there. I told him about how successful my evenings were and that I felt we could be of mutual benefit to each other. I laid it all out for him, trying to sell a vision of how the evenings would go, along the lines of 'Come and see Bobby George play darts and try the latest Courage beers'.

'Darts punters love their beer,' I assured him, as if he didn't know. 'I'll do everything else for you,' I said. 'I'll get myself a driver and bring a master of ceremonies [MC]. We can deck the place out in Courage colours and everything.'

He seemed fairly keen but I sensed there were still a couple of drawbacks.

'How much is this going to cost and how do I know you're any good; what have you won?' he enquired.

I was already getting a living wage from my floor-laying and was winning quite a lot of prize money, so felt that £200 a week would be a fair investment from Courage. I then told him about my win in the North American Open and all my other titles and also mentioned that I was the Essex county captain.

He still appeared to have a few doubts, so I told him that he could see for himself what he would be getting, as I would be on television this coming Saturday, playing in the finals of the *News of the World* Championship for the second year running.

'What, THE grand finals?' Now he was interested, wasn't he. That was the tournament everyone knew about. It was the National Darts Association World Championship really; no one ever recognised it as such, but they should have. The BDO

World Championships started in 1978 but the *News of the World* was the only nationwide tournament and it had been going for over 50 years by then.

I handed Dave my contact details and left him to consider my offer. Meanwhile, I had a date with destiny to prepare for – and a floor to finish!

There was, of course, a chance that I wouldn't even get seen on the telly if my match wasn't shown or if I was knocked out early on but darts was blessed with a huge stroke of fortune that particular Saturday afternoon. There was some sort of dispute which prevented ITV from showing the horse racing that day and suddenly they had lots of gaps to fill in their afternoon schedule. The original intention had been to show only the semi-finals and final of the darts but now they stayed with it and showed all the matches in full.

It was my second appearance at the *News of the World* finals and I vowed not to be distracted by it all, like I had been the previous year when I came up short in my first encounter with a prancing and preening Scotsman named Jocky Wilson. This time I knew what to expect, I'd got a little bit more experience under my belt and was also playing at the top of my game. I hadn't dropped a single leg en route to the finals and that would continue as I made my way through the field.

Every leg was won in 15 darts or fewer, the first time that anyone had averaged over 100 in winning a live televised event. My opponent, Alan Glazier, was gracious in defeat and when I left Wembley Arena with that beautiful trophy I knew that my life had changed for good.

First thing Monday morning I received a telephone call from Dave Clarke. 'Bloody hell, I didn't know you could play like that,' he said. 'I've been thinking about what you said about the idea of going round the pubs and clubs and I reckon it's something that Courage would be interested in doing. Was it £200 a week you were after?'

'Ha, it's gone up to £200 a night now,' I laughed, testing the water a little.

'I knew you were going to do that,' he said. And so began an association with the brewery that lasted for many years, although my personal terms improved very quickly.

Things were done properly; I made my own stage, bought an electronic scoreboard and sorted out my own driver and got Phil Jones or Freddie Williams, two of the top referees on the circuit, to MC most of the events for me.

When I worked in the north-east a chap called Roy 'Chubby' Brown worked with me. Heard of him? He can be a little bit naughty, even for a broad-minded darts audience, but we had some good times before he went off to do bigger and better things with his time.

Things were going along very nicely and I got a call to say that one of the Courage reps wanted to come along to one of the shows to see for himself. His name was Michael Jackson, who I immediately re-christened 'Whacko Jacko', a lovely man, who spoke a little bit like what I do. He lived in Newbury, so when we were doing a show in south Wales we arranged to pick him up on the way and take him with us. Once we'd got to the venue he watched on whilst I put out all the Courage banners, beer mats and bar towels, making the place look as professional as I could.

'You do all that yourself?' he asked.

'Yes, everything,' I told him. 'I just ask for bed and breakfast when we're staying over, otherwise I do all the setting up and pay for my own beer. I don't ask the company for an evening meal, a morning paper or anything extra; that was the agreement I had with Dave Clarke. I don't take liberties!' Whacko Jacko ended up on the road with me for the rest of that week and a few days after we got back I was asked to go in to head office to discuss my contract. One of the bigwigs from the company would be there and all the reps were told to attend.

I thought they were going to bring it all to an end or something but made the effort to look smart and off I toddled. In the hallway I saw Dave Clarke and asked him what it was all about and if the bloke in charge was a bit of a toff, would it be all blah, blah, blah, that kind of stuff.

'Oh no, he's alright, I think you'll like him,' said Dave.

In I went and everyone was sat round this beautifully polished oak table, loads of reps were sat down one side of it. It was only the boardroom, wasn't it. Then in came the bigwig and it turned out to be none other than Michael Jackson.

He introduced me to everyone and told them about the week he'd spent with me, then he asked his head of special promotions, a lovely lady called Sue Roberts, to set up a new contract for me.

They completely changed the structure of my agreement with them: they were offering me more money; reps were to be there, setting everything up; I was authorised to put all my beer on a Courage tab and it was also put into my contract that I was entitled to a meal at the end of each evening. Usually by that time only the Indian and Chinese restaurants were still open but that didn't matter, it was all taken care of.

In short, Whacko Jacko was so impressed by what he'd seen that he wanted me out there, almost full-time, flying the flag for Courage and he wanted to pay me good money to do it.

He arranged for me to be kitted out in Courage-branded polo shirts, jackets and trousers and for thousands of photographs and darts flights to be made available to give away to punters. In the space of a few short minutes he was effectively giving me the best contract anyone in darts could have.

They wanted their money's worth, though. I was out there five days a week for them, often doing two shows a day; one at lunch, say 11am until 3pm and then off to a hotel for a couple of hours' kip and then an evening somewhere else from 7.30 until closing time. One day they even wanted me to go all the way down to Plymouth, just to have my photo taken in my Courage gear alongside some of the big names at the Boat Show. They put me on very good money and two shows a day is double very good money. It was the same for whoever was driving me or doing the MC for the night – they were on double bubble as well. My days of laying floors were coming to an end.

ERIC, ONE OF A KIND

YOU'VE PROBABLY heard of Eric Bristow. He won the BDO World Championship on five occasions and we had a lot of battles together before becoming very good friends. We always brought the best out of each other and people still tell me nowadays that the 1980 world final between us was the one they most fondly remember or the one that got them into darts. I should have beaten him on that famous occasion at Jollees nightclub in Stoke-on-Trent but it wasn't to be; it was his day.

The first time I met him was whilst playing in a BDO event at Margate in Kent. I'd seen him around and knew he was a mouthy so-and-so but I taught him a lesson on that occasion. After the event was over some of us hung around and started playing for £1 a leg, winner stays on. I went on a streak, winning leg after leg and he was eager to play me.

He was told to put his name down and wait his turn, the same as everybody else. I could hear him telling everyone how good he was, so I waited until he was next in line and then deliberately lost my next match, to my mate Malcolm Ellis, who I'd gone on the fishing trip to Ireland with.

I'd already pocketed a few quid by then, so was more than happy. Even more so, when Eric then went and lost to Malcolm. He was fuming that he hadn't had the chance to play me after waiting so long.

After that we became good mates and he would do anything for me, anything. One night we were due to do an exhibition together and we were both coming from different directions. Chatting with Eric beforehand he said, 'There's very little parking there but if I get there first, I'll save you a space.'

On the night in question it was pouring with rain, absolutely chucking it down. It took me some time to find the venue but when I did, there was Eric, soaked to the skin, outside standing in a space preventing anyone else from parking there. 'Here you are Bo, told you I'd save you a space.' He was saturated but had been good to his word.

We both loved our darts and we used to go anywhere to try to make a few quid playing challenge matches, something we called 'money racing'. It meant going to an area and playing against the best players there for cash. No-nonsense stuff, winner takes all. It was a way of not only making a few quid but it also toughened your game, challenging yourself against the best.

It also helped you get known and at that stage I was happy to travel and play against anyone. If you went to, say, south Wales and played against Leighton Rees or Alan Evans in their backyard, in front of their mates and fans, you always emerged wiser for the experience.

Whilst I was still a raw novice in the game I would often go along with Eric to play in these matches or give him a bit of moral support. One afternoon he called me, asking me to pick him up that evening and take him to the Mother Hubbard pub, at Loughton in Essex. He'd been challenged to a money race and wasn't going to miss out on the opportunity to rub someone's nose in it and line his pockets at the same time.

Well, it didn't pan out like that. Bob Wood was a more than decent player and on this particular night he wiped the floor with Eric, he beat him up really bad. After he'd stopped cursing and moaning about how it had gone, my mate said, 'I suppose you'd better pay him.'

'You what?' I laughed. 'What do you mean, me pay him? You just told me to pick you up, I ain't paying him. I've not got much on me, what is it anyway?'

'200 notes,' he whispered.

'I've not got anywhere near that on me,' I confessed. 'You just told me to pick you up and take you back home.'

'Fuckin' hell,' he went. 'We're going to get our heads kicked in.' The place was packed and they were all going crazy and congratulating the winner. A lot of money was changing hands, with plenty of people having invested large wagers on the outcome.

One thing that I always admired about Eric in all the years I knew him was that he had a lot of bottle and could usually talk himself out of a scrape. This time though, it was at my expense.

He started baiting his conqueror, winding Bob Wood up by telling him that he'd got lucky. 'Let's see how good you really are, see if you can beat the big fella.'

As he was saying that he was pointing at me. Me!

Bob wasn't having it, he wanted his money but Eric kept drawing him in. 'If you're as good as you think you are you can double your money. Come on, double or nothing if you can beat Bobby.'

I'd been dropped right in the cart but there was no other way to get out of there without getting a good hiding. I looked around and nobody was going to be wanting me to win, I'd got no friends there. That was pressure.

The standard format for those matches was always best of seven legs, each of 1,001 and there wasn't much between us, but then I lost a bit of rhythm and realised I might be in a spot of trouble. As we neared the end he was outscoring me. If I hit 85 he was getting a ton or 140 and so on. He had a lead and I wasn't right on my game.

I slipped Eric the keys to my Ford Cortina and whispered, 'Go and get the engine started and leave the passenger door open. If he hits the winning double I'm running out of that door and you'd better be there, cos if we don't fuck off straight away we're going to get our heads kicked in.'

After I went up and had my next throw Eric was there, tugging at my shirt.

'What?' I asked him.

He looked pathetically at me and confessed, 'I can't drive.'

I couldn't believe it; what a wally. There was only one way out of this now and I was as focused as I've ever been on a dartboard. Hitting a string of 180s I turned the match around and you can imagine the relief when I won on the final leg.

Eric was shaking, I was covered in sweat and we both knew that we'd got out of a hole. It didn't matter at that point that we'd played all night for nothing but it was another invaluable learning experience. We even had a chuckle about it on the way home.

Even then I knew that Eric was going to be something special, on and off the board; he really was one of a kind.

Most of the time he would be good as gold until about 10 or 10.30pm, then he would become a complete arsehole. By then the drink had taken hold. He'd be rude, arrogant, leery and happy to pick a fight with anyone. I didn't like him when he was like that; no one did.

Next morning he'd be up and at it again, without a care in the world. 'Morning Bob, alright last night, wasn't it? Didn't show myself up, did I?'

I'd have to tell him he'd been a complete dick and would say that I'd had enough of it and that I wasn't going to do any more shows with him. We'd go on like an old married couple and he'd be all apologetic and promise it wouldn't happen again and you'd think he meant it, until the next time.

As his career progressed, so did the fallouts. Promoters would get sick of his antics and in the end he became a problem for them. Eric was such a big draw that people wanted to see him, meet him, play him. Then, of course, they'd all want to buy him a drink.

The vicious circle would inevitably lead to more trouble later on, so he'd get stuck on first at exhibitions and then sent on his way before anything happened.

There's no doubt he was one of the greats of the game and for a while he ruled the roost. He would win most things and as his buddy it would be fairly lucrative for me because we would share prize money. When we went around together, if he didn't win tournaments, then I would and we'd clean up in the pairs together.

On one occasion it seemed that Lady Luck wasn't going to let us win, no matter how well we thought we were playing. Eric and I had reached the final of the Oxford pairs, playing on an old elm board. I went up first to throw: bounce out, bounce out, bounce out. Incredible. The crowd began to get involved, hoping the local pairing that we were up against might now go on and win.

After their first throw Eric went to the board. He was at the top of his game, a lovely wrist action with his trademark little pinky sticking out. His first dart unluckily hit the wire and dropped to the floor, as did the second dart and then the third. We couldn't believe it and in truth no one else could. What were the odds on that? Me and him, two of the top-ranked players in the world scoring nil after six darts.

The crowd were lapping it up and booing Eric, so he snatched the microphone off the MC and said, 'Never mind booing, there's no one else in here could do that, so shaaaat up!'

Fortunately, we overcame our poor start and went on to win the title and pocketed the prize money again.

The first time I stepped on an aeroplane was with Eric and a number of the other top British players as we embarked on a tour of the USA in 1978. It had been put together by Paul Durrant, owner of the Durro darts manufacturing company, who paid for our flights but would be reimbursed with some of the prize money if we were to win any.

Leighton Rees, John Lowe, Tony Brown, Tony Sontag, Colin Baker, Denis Ovens and two of the top female players, Pat Piper and Linda Batten, all made the trip, as did BDO chief Olly Croft.

I was unsure about giving up almost a month of my time but was encouraged to go on the trip by an employer at the time, Roy Cottee. 'Have a crack, Bob,' he told me. 'You'll always be able to lay floors but you might not have an opportunity to make it as a darts player again.'

The trip turned into a goldmine for us all and I was able to claim the biggest prize of the lot by winning the North American Open. It was an annual event, held on the cruise liner, *Queen Mary I*, permanently moored off Long Beach in California. Battling my way through a 512-strong field, I defeated the American Pete Polinski in the final.

Eric even volunteered to chalk that match for us and leapt higher than I did when I hit the winning double. This was a major breakthrough for me and apart from the title and the $4,000 winner's cheque, it also guaranteed me a place in the Winmau World Masters at Wembley.

It was one of a number of successes over that month in the USA and if I wasn't winning, then one of the other Brits would be and in every sense it turned out to be a hugely profitable venture. I loved going back there for the tournaments and one year Eric and I were cleaning up, going all around the country winning the open tournaments and making decent money as one or other of us won the singles and between us we'd be virtually unbeatable in the pairs.

We were somewhere over on the West Coast and were both playing really well as we eased our way through the draw into the final of a pairs competition. They were crafty how they organised those things – all the names were written on cards and the pile was then split into two and the draw was then done by just taking one card off each pile. Along with the other British lads, we'd noticed that wherever we went, there had been a careful bit of seeding, with all the top American players kept apart from us to make sure they'd always have representation in the final.

True to form, on this particular day, we'd battled our way through and found ourselves up against a couple of the home hopefuls. Eric was incensed about the way they'd done it and more so when the MC started the stage announcements.

'Ladies and gentlemen, our final is England versus the United States of America.'

'No, it fucking ain't,' snarled my mate.

Flags were then paraded and placed on the chairs on each side of the stage. The American Stars and Stripes was cheered to the rafters and some pantomime booing greeted the arrival of the Union flag.

Eric wasn't having any of that. Quite rightly, he pointed out that the Union flag wasn't a fair representation as we were both English and in any case we were playing for ourselves, not our national team. But the organisers continued to ignore him and just carried on regardless.

'Right, England to throw first, game on,' said the MC.

That riled Eric some more and part of me thought he was getting unnecessarily worked up over it but I also knew it would inspire his game if he felt there was a wrong to be righted.

I started and got a decent score, a ton or a 140 and Eric whispered, 'Fuck this, I'm only throwing for bulls and 25s.'

True to his word, he hit a couple of bullseyes and a 25 with his first throw and over the course of the final I've never seen such sustained accuracy on the middle target, at least one bull every throw, sometimes two and on a couple of occasions he banged in all three.

He was loving it, really taking the piss. Whenever we got near to a finish I would take it out, except for the final leg when I deliberately left him 50, which he finished in one dart, of course. Boom, we'd won again but my mate wouldn't let it lie there.

He marched over to the other side of the stage, picked up the US flag and pretended to wipe his arse with it before chucking it on the floor. I couldn't believe it. You should have heard the crowd, they went ballistic and started to advance towards the stage. They were booing and gesturing towards him.

'You fucking arsehole,' they shouted at him. 'We're gonna get you for that.' The atmosphere had turned really toxic and

I was worried that someone was going to do something really stupid, like pull a gun out on him, or something.

'Watch yourself, Eric,' I whispered in his ear. 'These guys aren't messing about and they have guns over here!'

At that he just disappeared off the stage, went out the back and buggered off, leaving me stood there to face the music, apologise on his behalf and collect the trophies and prize money. I didn't see him again until I got back to the hotel, where he was full of it.

He'd gone over the top; you can't disrespect another nation's flag like that, especially when you're in their country and when they've all had a few drinks. But my word, how well he played that day. I didn't believe he'd stick to throwing for the bull but he was incredible. I'd like to say that was an isolated incident but it wasn't. That's how he was, always getting into trouble but somehow always managing to get himself out of it.

From experience I know what a pain he was to play against but he was great to play alongside or to have in your corner. He loved a battle and was always up for it, especially when we played for England.

I can remember one year we were up in Scotland and we were 11-0 up against the old enemy. There were 12 singles matches and we needed just one more victory to complete a whitewash. Can you believe it? That wasn't going down too well with the partisan Scots and the mood in the hall was pretty sour. There was only one issue: yours truly had been drawn to play last.

Coaxed by Eric, the rest of the England team got up close to the stage and made sure that I knew what was at stake. A clean sweep at that level is pretty rare but everyone else had taken care of business and now all the pressure was on me to emulate them.

As I was throwing my practice darts, the first voice I heard was Eric's.

'Don't you lose, you c**t.'

The bastard. If it wasn't bad enough getting barracked by several hundred very agitated Scots, I was also getting it from my own team-mates. They weren't concerned for long and I ended up giving them all a poke in the eye because I not only won easily but also took the Man of the Match award for getting the best average of the day in sealing the 12-0 win.

Those international encounters in Scotland weren't for the faint-hearted and one year things really got out of hand.

Paul Gosling was playing for us – I like Paul a lot, he's a big, funny guy and they were booing him throughout, so he put his middle finger up to them. That was typical Paul but not really the wisest course of action on this particular day.

They started chucking beer cans at him. Full cans at that, so he picked one up, opened it and necked the contents before giving them another sight of his middle finger. Have that!

It wasn't a day for seeing the humour in his actions. Another load of cans came flying towards him and then someone threw a big green ashtray which splintered everywhere as it hit the stage. That was bad, that spoilt it and it was ages before order was restored and the match could be continued. Paul got into a bit of trouble and had to sit out the next couple of matches because of his reaction.

No mention of Scottish darts would be complete without a word on Kirkcaldy's finest, former World Champion John Thomas Wilson. Our first meeting hadn't gone well for me when he'd beaten me in my first *News of the World* grand finals but after that we became great mates and played together in quite a lot of pairs events over the years. He also saved my life, which we'll come on to later.

Most of the time he'd be good as gold, so polite and respectful. If a lady came into a room Jocky would stand up straight away and offer her a chair. There was the other side of him, of course. Once he'd had a few drinks he'd turn into a right pisshead and wouldn't shy away from any trouble, particularly if it became an England v Scotland thing.

He'd start on, 'You, you, see you, you fucking English …' He'd stare at me like I'd nicked his pint. And he was supposed to be my mate. When he was drunk he was a fucking nuisance but he didn't even need to have a drink inside him before he would lose his rag with Eric or the Welsh star, Alan Evans.

Those three always seemed to rub each other up the wrong way and the BDO coffers were often swelled by their inability to get on. Some of their confrontations were legendary and it wasn't just put on for the television cameras.

Away from the aggro, huge laughs were always on the menu whenever I caught up with (Big) Cliff Lazarenko, a real character and a formidable opponent. He was good enough – and unfortunate enough – to reach four World Championship semi-finals without making the final.

I beat him in his first in 1980, a year later he got revenge by beating me at the quarter-final stage but then he couldn't get past Eric. Later he lost to John Lowe in 1985 and to Phil Taylor five years later.

With a little more fortune, Cliff could quite easily have been a World Champion. On his day he was as tough as anyone to beat and we had some great times rooming together, either at the big tournaments or on England duty.

DOING MY BIT FOR THE COUNTRY

LIFTING THE North American Open title was a real lift-off moment for me, a clinical victory in a field full of the best players in the world. It was my first top-class triumph and had come within two years of throwing my first dart. None of it made sense really and looking back, it seems even more of a remarkable achievement now than it did then.

Whilst that day at Long Beach was further vindication that I was right to concentrate on my new career path, I also quickly found out that I had much to learn after unwittingly getting caught up in some behind-the-scenes politics. I allowed myself to get sucked into an argument that didn't really have anything to do with me and I should have distanced myself from immediately.

A deal had been struck by the BDO for the sports manufacturer Admiral to provide the shirts for all forthcoming England international sides. Many of the players that were involved weren't happy about the exclusivity that they were after. Anyway, a few of them obviously set me up.

It's always very noticeable that when someone wins something – be it in darts or any other walk of life – everyone wants to know them and be around them and tell them how good they are. I was happy to be having some beers with Eric Bristow, John Lowe and Tony Brown – some of the biggest stars of the England side at the time – and they mentioned that it wouldn't be long now before I would be selected for my international debut. Whilst that may or may not have been true, I was more than happy to be the centre of attention and bask in the glow of my win, without noticing that I was being buttered up.

Gradually the subject of shirt sponsorship came around and it was obvious that there was some discontent that the England players couldn't have their own sponsors' names on the new Admiral shirts as well. I was sponsored by Durro at the time and could see their point: it would be nice if I was playing for my country, to have them recognised on the shirt also. The others were adamant that they wouldn't play under the proposed restrictions and wondered if I could broach the subject with Olly Croft, the BDO guv'nor.

Old silly bollocks here didn't even pause to think about it but went and told Olly that he'd got a problem on his hands because no one would play for England anymore if they couldn't have their own sponsor on the team shirts.

Understandably I was feeling quite proud of myself. I was the North American Open champion and my 'soon-to-be' England team-mates (or so I thought) had so much faith in me that they'd elected me as their spokesman for such a big issue.

Was I gullible or what?

'Oh, is that right?' said Olly. 'Are you sure about that, lad?'

What happened? I was obviously seen as a potential troublemaker and didn't get within a mile of the England side for another couple of years, whilst the others got picked as normal. How naïve I'd been. You can't trust some people, you know. They'd done me right up like a kipper.

It wasn't until I'd become number one in the world rankings that I was able to force my way into the England side, eventually winning 25 caps for my country, although but for injury and my own stupidity it should have been a lot more.

At least I did get the chance to play international darts, something that my good friend Lil Coombes was never able to experience despite being the best in the world at one time.

Like myself, Lil was a late bloomer with regards to darts, taking it up when she was 55. From Felixstowe, we played county darts with Suffolk together and I could see how good she was. Lil was a very independent woman and could be very humorous to be around. However, when she was on the oche she was quite feisty and wanted to beat everyone up. She was a steady player and regularly hit 180s and 140s.

Over time, we played a lot of mixed pairs' together and one year she went off to Helsinki to play in the Finland Open but didn't have a partner for the mixed pairs. I wasn't intending to be at that one but she rang me at home and asked if I would fly up there and partner her, assuring me that all expenses would be met by her sponsor and that the prize money was very good. The only issue was that all available accommodation had been snapped up, so I'd have to share a hotel room with Lil – but at least it contained a double bed!

There was nothing else for it and I had no other options, so Lil and I bunked down and shared the only available bed left in the place. I think she was about 70 at the time. As you could imagine, word quickly got around and I lost count of the number of times that players thought they were being original when they came up and whispered, 'Hope Lil was on the pill!'

Anyway, it all turned out well because we won the mixed pairs and the prize money turned out to be better than the men's events, much to the annoyance of Eric, who hadn't bothered entering.

By that stage of her career Lil's chances of playing for England had gone but when she was about 61 or 62 she was the best around and top of the world rankings. It was scandalous that she never got an opportunity to play for her country but knowing what happened to me, I'm not surprised. I suspect it was purely an age thing that prevented her from being selected.

Being a late starter, I never took anything for granted in darts and it was always such a huge honour for me to be called up to represent my country. I tried to make the most of every opportunity but there was one occasion when it turned to my advantage not to be selected.

In every sense, I've done a lot for breweries over the years and the reps all have my number. Being particularly close to some of the Greene King guys, towards the end of 1982 I was asked about the chances of getting something organised for television – a four-man international team event to be screened live, between England and a Rest of the World side.

This sounded like fun but giving a firm commitment to it was way out of my league; it all came under the auspices of the BDO and, in particular, Olly Croft, so I steered the brewery in his direction very quickly. Details were exchanged and it was all systems go, for some time early in 1983, to be played in Ipswich or somewhere around the Suffolk area, the home of Greene King breweries.

Everything was set – the venue, the teams, broadcasters recording it, tickets sold. One thing that hadn't been factored in during the negotiating stage was that a couple of weeks before the event, the sport gained a new World Champion, with Keith Deller defeating Eric in the final. That was Ipswich's Keith Deller, of course.

I turned up on the night and we were all excited and then I saw Olly Croft coming towards me. He'd obviously found himself backed into a very difficult situation and must have been dreading the conversation that unfolded.

'Do you mind if Deller plays instead of you, Bobby?'

I told him that I didn't go a deal on it; this was shaping up to be a big event and with the television coverage it would do me a lot of good if I was seen to be playing well.

'Look,' said Olly, 'we'll still pay you £1,000, the same as the others are getting, how's that then?'

I had to check what I was hearing, but he confirmed that I was essentially being paid to NOT play for my country. As long as I was getting the 'bees and honey' I wasn't that bothered and in a lot of ways it made sense: Deller was the new World Champion, the golden boy and Greene King had their local hero to promote, while the rest of the team had been picked on the latest world rankings, with Eric, Lowey and Tony Brown ahead of me at the time. And I'd get a backhander to stay out of it.

Keeping the news to myself, I joined the others in the back room, sort of a football changing room, waiting for the event to start. I was sat on a wooden bench next to Eric, and Olly walked in and gave me an envelope. Eric didn't like missing out on anything so was at it straight away, head swivelling like a meerkat, 'What's that then, what's he given you there, mate?'

His response was predictable once I'd told him what had happened, although he didn't believe me at first.

'Faaaack orf, you're joking, you're having me on,' he said, so I opened up the envelope and showed him the cheque.

The news was quickly spread around the players. 'What do you think of this, Bobby's getting paid and he's not even going to chuck a dart.'

'That's out of order,' someone piped up.

They only quietened down when I reminded them that it was nothing to do with me and that I'd turned up, the same as they had, expecting to play. It was only fair that I was paid for my trouble.

Things had just about calmed down but then the rep from Greene King walked in and thanked me for my help in getting it all organised.

'No problem,' I said. 'I was just happy to help out.'

'Yes, I know,' he went on. 'But we hear that Olly's had a word and I understand you've graciously agreed to stand down so Keith can play. That's very kind of you, so we'd like to give you this.'

It was another envelope and another cheque for £1,000.

Eric went ballistic and I just poured oil on the fire, saying, 'Fucking hell mate, I must be famous. Two grand and I don't even have to throw a dart!'

'STUFF HIM E!'

IT WOULDN'T be the most controversial thing I ever uttered if I said that women's darts has improved dramatically in recent years. Some of the players nowadays can quite rightly be regarded as world class and are more than capable of holding their own against most in the men's game.

Lisa Ashton for one is an incredible player and I love how she just gets on with it. No nonsense, she gets up there, throws 180s for fun, retrieves her darts straight away and gets on with it. No histrionics, no messing about, no game play, she's just a great player and a lovely lady as well.

I was asked on television if she reminded me of anyone in the men's game and saw that as an opportunity for a cheap laugh.

'Yes,' I said. 'She throws like Steve Beaton but the good thing is she doesn't look anything like him!' I must apologise to Steve for that as I love him to bits but it was funny at the time.

The likes of Lisa and Trina Gulliver and Deta Hedman have dominated the women's game for some time but the next generation is coming through. Beau Greaves looks as if she is going to have an outstanding career and we've already seen what Fallon Sherrock can do at the highest level. Together, they've dramatically raised the profile of women's darts and are looking to find the consistency to have many years of success.

As I suggested at the start, it wasn't always like that.

I captained Essex between 1976 and 1986 and my labouring skills came in handy back then because I made the stage set-up for them. It must have looked OK because other counties asked me to do something similar for them and I made set-ups for London, Yorkshire and the England team.

The late Pat Williams, who was the wife of well-known darts MC and caller Freddie Williams, ran the Essex women's team and she wondered why I was about to turn the board between the women's match ending and the men's match starting.

'Why are you doing that?' she enquired. 'The treble-20 bed looks fine to me.'

'It is,' I agreed. 'But the 1 is worn out!'

I gave her a wink to let her know I was joking but she did her nut and went complaining to the committee about my attitude. They knew I'd said it tongue-in-cheek but had to be seen to do something, so sent me a letter asking me not to run the ladies' team down.

Pat and I had some right spats over the years. I called her 'Bossy Boots' but generally we rubbed along alright for most of the time. Her husband Freddie was my MC for a period, so she came along and helped set the gear up and do the scoring. I was appreciative of that but in the end she wore me down and was responsible for me leaving my home county, Essex, on a matter of principle.

Turning up for a county match one day I was stopped on the door of the venue by Pat, who always seemed to try to make things difficult where I was concerned.

'Where are you going?' she asked at the door.

'I'm going in, where do you think I'm going?' I replied.

'It's £1, everyone's got to pay £1,' Pat stated.

Now, I'm not hard up for a quid, nor am I indifferent to a reasonable request, but I don't go a lot on being told what to do, without any rhyme or reason.

'What's it for?' I enquired.

She went on to say that everyone must pay £1 for a programme, to help cover costs and all sorts of stuff. Now if this had gone through the committee or we'd been asked politely, then there wouldn't have been an issue, but on this particular day I wasn't having it.

I'd played for Essex for ten years and was proud to be their captain and because of my association with Courage I'd been able to bring in sponsorship money worth £25,000 spread over five years.

Old 'Bossy Boots' wanted a quid. Well, she wasn't getting it and nor did she get it from any of the other players, who walked away with me that day. Afterwards I played my county darts for Suffolk for a while, later I joined London then returned to Suffolk to be able to play alongside my son Richard.

It was during my time with Suffolk that I met a bloke who has become a good mate over the years, although at first sight I wondered if he was a sandwich short of a picnic.

A decent little county player, Andriy Iwan Batih – AKA Andy Bathie – liked yellow. And when I say he liked yellow – he really did like the colour yellow. Whenever he was around you'd find him wearing one of his bright yellow shirts.

That was too good an opportunity for me to ignore, so dear old Andriy became 'Tweety Pie' and the nickname stuck. Over 30 years later everyone still knows him as Tweety (although the grandchildren call him Twatty!) but at least he's forgiven me and has become part of the family. He's always been there for us, just like our lovely Mrs Claus – Pat Reeve – who has come round to help look after the place since we've been at George Hall. She always used to do the lawns and gardens for us, with her late partner Dave Clarke (not the Courage Brewery Dave Clarke!) and they always brought gifts round for the boys. Robert and Richard called them Santa and Mrs Claus – and the name has stuck. Pat used to run Essex youth even before Richard started playing for them. We're so lucky to have her.

Back to women's darts, which is where we were before we went off on a lemon-coloured and Mrs Claus detour. What a brilliant player Maureen Flowers was. She was the dominant force in the women's game for more than a decade from the mid-1970s and was always the one to be avoided in the draw. In 1980 we were all over in the USA and Maureen had a great run through the field at the Santa Monica Open and met me in the semi-finals. This was an open tournament, don't forget, with most of the world's best men playing in it, so that tells you something about how good she was.

At that time Maureen was in a steady relationship with Eric, who had already won his semi-final and clearly fancied playing his girlfriend in the final. It was best of three and she took the first leg off me. I thought, 'oh for fuck's sake Bobby, don't get beaten by Eric's girlfriend, you'll never hear the end of it'.

I could hear Eric getting excited at the prospect: 'Come on Mo, stuff him,' he kept blaring out.

As it happens, I quickly got my act together and came back and won the last two legs quite easily to set up a mouthwatering clash in the final against Eric.

Then it started. 'Come on E, stuff him,' Maureen was shouting out now, exactly the same as he had done earlier. They made a fine double act, that pair.

One other thing I remember from that match was our throwing for the bullseye – it must have been the longest on record. I'm sure you're aware before a match the two players will throw to see who goes first. Both will have a dart at the bullseye and the nearest to it gets the choice. Over a short format game it's obviously very important to throw first.

On this particular occasion, neither player wanted to miss out. If I hit a bull Eric did; if I hit the 25 so did he. We went on for ages: bull bull, 25 25, bull bull, bull bull, 25 25, 25 25.

Eventually I won it for the right to throw first and went on to narrowly win the match and the title. Don't underestimate the importance of throwing first.

Of the Brits that made the trip across to play in all those American events that year, four of us, Tony Sontag, Leighton Rees, Eric and myself, had been splitting any prize money we won. We then went on to the Los Angeles Open and the four of us won the team event quite easily, then myself and Tony Sontag won the pairs and Eric and Maureen triumphed in the mixed doubles.

Again, Eric and I were due to meet in the final of the singles but he announced beforehand that he didn't want to share the prize money any more. Fair enough, I said, you'll be out of pocket. I went on to beat him for the second time in the week and made a point of putting the prize money into the pot but I gave Tony Eric's share as well.

It was decent money, too – the USA tournaments regularly paid out $1,000 to the winner, which was a lot back then. Every time I went across the pond I seemed to lift most of the prizes, especially the team event, even though I often played with a different set of lads.

One year Eric, Leighton, Jocky and me were breezing our way through to the final of the North American Open team event. Best of three legs, 801, we weren't going to lose many games with that line-up, were we? Four of the top-ranked players in the world, well three and a half...!

Upon reaching the final Eric piped up, 'Let's make it interesting, if anyone hits a 180 it's $50 a man. The other three have to cough up.'

I threw for the bull, won it and started with a 180. Bang, bang, bang, lovely. Thank you, gentlemen, that will be $50 apiece. At the back of the stage, money was being passed around from hand to hand and I'm nicely in profit, thank you very much.

Next up to throw for us was Eric. Boom, 180 from him as well, so I gave him his money back and both Leighton and Jocky had to put their hand in their pocket once again. Then it was Leighton's turn and he also hit 180, so he got his money back as well.

Poor old Jocky, he hadn't thrown a dart and had paid out three times in a row but now it was his turn. He went to the board and hit 45. We were in fits of laughter because he went off on one: 'This is a fucking conspiracy, this is,' he snarled. 'You're all ganging up on me.'

Wiping the tears from my eyes, I called him a fucking idiot. 'But I'm down $150 Bobby,' he wailed. 'Well hit one yourself then,' I told him. We easily won the match, so at least the wee fella had some prize money to console himself with.

We actually got a ticking off at the end of the match from Tom Fleetwood, who was the executive director and co-founder of the American Darts Organisation. A giant of a man, weighing in at something over 30 stone, he had a massive, powerful voice and he came over to us and said, 'No more gambling gentlemen please, we are playing the final of the North American Fours, no more gambling on this stage.'

We just sniggered at him. We'd cleaned up by then and three of us had managed to get some extra pocket money out of John Thomas Wilson.

IN BED WITH THE ARROW

DARTS IS played virtually all over the globe nowadays but that wasn't always the case. Rothmans cigarettes helped spread the word by sponsoring some of us to go on a tour of the Middle East, where we played in Sharjah, Abu Dhabi and Dubai. Jocky Wilson was on that trip and I'll always remember him getting burnt to a cinder.

The sponsors had given us some Bermuda shorts for the trip but the wee man had just stuffed his into his suitcase without trying them on for size. When it came to us having a relaxing time beside the pool, Jocky discovered that he'd been given some shorts that would have been about right for Big Cliff: they were enormous. He looked ridiculous but didn't care and laid there, without sun cream, getting redder by the minute. I didn't help by telling him that it was a local custom where you couldn't get served at the bar if you didn't have a full set of teeth. Remarkably, the gap-toothed Scot believed me and went thirsty!

Bill Lennard was also with us for that trip; a lovely man and a very decent player. From Manchester, Bill was also a winner of the *News of the World* Championship, having defeated Leighton

Rees in the 1976 final. He was also my opponent the first time I got through to the final of the Butlins Grand Masters.

People tend to forget about that tournament but at the time it was one of the most prestigious events. It was played over two nights in Birmingham and then shown once a week on the ITV network over a period of two or three months, so the players and the audience were all sworn to secrecy and couldn't tell anyone who'd won until it had been screened.

Only the very best in the world competed in it and I was lucky enough to win it twice, beating Bill in the 1979 final and Leighton a year later. I really fancied my chances of making it three in a row but during the 1981 event my back went and I had to pull out halfway through. That really was the start of my back problems.

John Lowe was a good darts player over a number of years, winning the BDO World Championship on three occasions. He and I never really got on but that's not surprising: everything that you associate me with, he was totally against it. 'Old Stoneface' as he was known, didn't like any form of change and thought everything should be exactly how he wanted it to be. From the outset he didn't like anyone who went against that, particularly me and everything I stood for. He didn't want to see any sparkly shirts or have anyone with a bit of personality sharing the stage with him. If there was any limelight to be had, he wanted it.

And don't get me started on the music. Could you imagine him playing nowadays in a big arena in the Premier League?

'Could you ask them to keep the noise down please, ref?'

Some might argue that the bigger events have got a little out of hand, especially with the jeering and booing when a player is on a finish but can you imagine nowadays if the players just made their way from the practice room and walked out on to the stage in deadly silence? I think the razzmatazz of the introductions and each player's individual music and flashy shirts are all part of the theatre and I was the first to do that, much to Mr Lowe's obvious annoyance. He was always going on about me and my capers and said he was going to get a union to put a stop to sequinned shirts and clowning around on the oche; I told him that I was going to form one myself, to ban wigs and false teeth. He didn't talk to me for about ten years after that!

I don't know why he was like he was. I've worked with him for years and tried to understand him but we're different characters and it's not to be. I'm not over-keen on him and I know he feels the same about me.

One of Lowey's best mates on the circuit was Tony Brown, a good, steady player who, like Cliff, reached the World Championship semi-finals on four occasions. I beat him a few times and he beat me a few times. Despite him hanging out a lot with Lowey, I didn't hold that against him and enjoyed his company. Although he was usually a pretty quiet bloke, he had a dry sense of humour and I mostly remember the good times we had on our trips abroad together.

When he travelled, he always brought along two suitcases: one was for his clothes and the other one was full of all sorts of medication, tablets, potions, plasters, bandages, cream, you name it, he'd got it. I wasn't feeling too well one evening and Tony said, 'Come with me, I'll sort it out.' We went to his room and he opened up his case. It was full of stuff and from then on I always called him Dr Brown.

Darts had burst out of the pubs and working men's clubs and on to the television screens during the mid to late 1970s. Fred Trueman's *Indoor League*, a weekly show that ran for five years and featured a variety of pub games including darts, bar billiards, arm wrestling, pool, table skittles and shove ha'penny, had shown that there was a market out there and suddenly some of the top players of the era became household names. Many were great characters, including the Welsh pair of Leighton Rees and Alan Evans, who were at the very inception of this new boom in the ratings. Thick as thieves they were, the pair of them. Great mates and fierce competitors.

I didn't really have that much to do with Leighton. If we were together, we'd get along fine but we didn't tend to hang out socially all that often and when we did he always seemed to be a little distant with me. His mate was a different kettle of fish. I got on very well with Alan and thought he was alright, quite a funny guy to be around. Everyone knew there was another side to him and that he could be a bit fiery if someone wound him up, but he never tried to take any liberties with me and wouldn't have got very far if he had.

I liked his sense of humour and he loved laughing at his own jokes. We were set to play an exhibition together in London somewhere and he was driving across from Wales.

'What time do you think you'll get here?' I asked him. Alan said that he didn't really know because of all the traffic, so I wrote down the name of a pub and told him I'd be in there from about 2pm and would wait in there for him. When I pitched up he was already there.

'Christ,' I said. 'How did you get here so fast?'

He drew me in nicely, 'I put my toe down and passed John Lowe on the M4.'

'Lowey?' I fell into his trap.

'Yeah. He was doing a ton but I was doing 180!'

Judging by the amount of joy he got from telling me that gag, I reckon he'd spent the entire journey thinking it up.

There's some wonderful footage that has survived of 'The Arrow' as they called him in the Rhondda. He was a wonderful player but also had a short fuse and was prone to flare-ups on stage, particularly against the likes of Jocky Wilson and Eric Bristow. After he beat Eric in the quarter-finals of the 1979 World Championship, they weren't particularly complimentary about each other on live television. Eric seldom went over the top in congratulating anyone who'd beaten him and couldn't believe he'd lost to the little Welshman. He weighed in with his assessment of Alan's chances of leaving with the trophy.

'You've got as much chance of winning this as you have of frying a pork chop in a synagogue,' was his considered opener.

'Well,' smiled the flamboyant Welshman. 'Put it this way Mr Bristow, I've got more chance of winning it than you because I've just beaten you.'

I got on alright with Alan and on one occasion I agreed to go down to Wales and do an exhibition with him. His dad had a pub near to where we were playing, so I stayed the night there.

'My dad's got a pub near to where we're playing,' he stated. 'You can stay there overnight, no problem.'

I met him at the venue and we had a good night and then headed back up the road to his dad's for a nightcap or two. 'What room is Bobby in, Dad?' asked Alan.

'Oh no, sorry son, I've let all the rooms out,' was a reply I didn't want to hear. I'd had a few drinks and was certainly in no state to be driving. 'Well, I can't go anywhere now, I'll just kip in the car or something,' I told them.

Alternative arrangements were quickly suggested, resulting in me sharing Alan's big double bed with him. As I said to my little Welsh mate at the time, 'It's better than nothing!'

Alan was good for the game of darts and lifted both the World Masters and British Open titles at the height of his career. He was a power scorer and mustard on the 180s but not quite as good on the doubles when it really mattered. We got on well and I always enjoyed working with him.

In 2022 I was asked to narrate a documentary about him for BBC Wales called *Alan 'The Arrow' Evans*, a tribute to one of the greats of the early period of televised darts. It brought back a lot of wonderful memories about a great period for the sport.

THE GRAND CHAMPION

ONE OF my best pals in the game was Alan Glazier, the left-handed English international who was known as either 'The Ton Machine' or 'The Man in Black'. Salt of the earth, he was a lovely guy and I was really shocked when he died during COVID in 2020. He'd gone to hospital to have his ticker done, at the age of 81. A few days after he'd had it sorted, I gave him a call on the mobile to see how he was getting on.

'Yeah, I'm alright Bo,' he said. 'They've put a stent in. I'm good, I feel a lot better now.'

I was pleased for him but then heard he was back in hospital, so gave him another call. 'What are you doing back in there?' I asked.

'Got COVID haven't I,' said Alan. 'Caught it last time I was in here.'

That was the last time I spoke to him, as two days later he'd died. I was absolutely gutted. What a sad way for such a lovely fella to go. He was always great company and so polite; the sort of guy that if you accidentally trod on his toes he'd be the one to say sorry.

A good time was guaranteed if you were on a night out with him; he was like a maverick from the cowboy days. Not averse to a few drinks and a game of cards, he was a magnet for the pretty girls to flock around.

On the dartboard he couldn't be underestimated either and fate was to pitch us both together for one of the biggest occasions of our lives. As a previous winner of the North American Open and the Swedish Open, Alan was one of the fancied picks for the 1979 *News of the World* Championship and stormed through the field. I was only glad that we managed to avoid each other until the final. Mates or not, there wasn't going to be any letting up from me on that particular afternoon at Wembley Arena as I swept him aside with two 15-dart legs to lift the coveted trophy.

'Bloody hell, you really wanted that,' he stated as he congratulated me. 'I couldn't get anywhere near you.'

I was overjoyed of course, but couldn't help feeling that if I hadn't won it that day then it would have been great to see Alan lift the famous old trophy.

In truth, I don't think there's anything that Alan – or anyone else – could have done to beat me that day. Throughout the entire qualifying tournament, on the way to the Grand Final, I didn't drop a single leg and on the day itself I averaged over 100 in each match, the first player to do that on television.

It was such a hard title to win, being played over such a short format. There were over 14,000 spectators present inside Wembley Arena, so I think there was even more pressure on my shoulders than when I was playing for England. The best of three legs, played from a throwing distance of 8ft, the *News of the World* was unique. It wasn't a formula that suited most players, but I'd played from that distance always from when I'd taken up the game just a few short years earlier.

I used to play from 8ft in my local pub and when I started doing exhibitions, I put the oche down at 8ft and no one could get anywhere near me. The standard BDO throw in those days was still 7ft 6in and blokes who had been playing for years were so used to it, they struggled at the longer mark. When I did all my exhibitions for Courage Breweries, I always put the oche down at 8ft. Some opponents would say, 'That's too long!' I'd say it wasn't. Fuck 'em. If I could throw from 8ft, then they should as well. Everyone throws from the shorter distance of 7ft 9.25in these days; it's the standard distance.

Some of you lads may say that 2.75in is not a lot. But ask your wife; if I had an extra 2.75in, I wouldn't have spent my time playing darts.

What a competition the *News of the World* Championship was. In its heyday it was THE darts competition that everyone wanted to win because it featured the best players in the world and couldn't be won by pure chance. Even after he'd become World Champion Eric's dad used to tease him that he'd not won anything until he'd won the *News of the World*. Perhaps that's why he was so happy when he eventually lifted it in 1983, four years after my first win.

The first time I can really recall being aware of the *News of the World* Championship was soon after I'd started throwing and met a fella called Ronnie Hayward in my local. Ronnie was an excellent player and liked a smoke. One day I noticed that he lit his cigarette with this magnificent silver lighter. It had the words '*News of the World*' and an image of a dartboard on it. It looked lovely and I asked him about it. He'd been presented with it for getting through to the area finals of the competition. He told me all about the event and how it had been his dream to walk out of Wembley holding the trophy aloft.

'If you win that you're the best player in the world,' he told me.

We'd become good friends and I think he was quietly impressed by my ability on the dartboard. He offered me the lighter.

'Do you want it?' he asked, seriously.

I was taken aback but I could see it was Ronnie's pride and joy.

'No thanks,' I said. 'I want the trophy!'

From then on, my sights were firmly set on giving it a good shot to try to win it. I'd missed the deadline for the 1977 event but in 1978 I stormed my way through the local, area, county and regional rounds to take my place amongst the 13 qualifiers for the most famous trophy in the sport.

Eric Bristow and his dad came to support me, along with a host of friends and regulars from the King George V in Ilford. I'd been made one of the favourites, alongside England international Tony Brown, but the draw pitted me against someone else I was to become more acquainted with in the near future, the Scottish qualifier named Jocky Wilson. Eric had already had some encounters with him and told me what to expect but my preparations were totally torn to shreds just before I was due to go on stage when the organisers told me I must change my shirt. The darts manufacturers Durro had sponsored me through the regional rounds and given me a shirt to wear, which included their logo. I was told it didn't meet the regulations and that I couldn't wear it. Farcically, a chap in the crowd offered to swap shirts with me, so I quickly whipped my top off and put his on instead, just before making my way on to the stage. Have you ever heard anything like it?

Jocky was buzzing around, like Eric warned me, but I can't use his antics or the change of shirt as an excuse. He beat me fair and square and my dream of becoming champion had fallen at the first hurdle. Eric called me a prat and I couldn't disagree with him.

At the time it seemed that my chance of winning that trophy had gone for good. I knew how difficult it had been to qualify and in every sense the achievement of reaching the grand finals in my first full year of playing darts had been astonishing. But now I wanted it even more and in 1979 all my dreams came true. Not only that, so did those of Ronnie Hayward, as I let him walk out of Wembley holding that trophy aloft. One or two spectators, worse the wear for drink, I'm sure, came and congratulated him on his victory!

Once I did a Q and A afternoon with Rod Harrington, who was very kind and introduced me as 'the Best 8ft Player in the World'. My record certainly backs that up: twice the *News of the World* champion, plus another three or four trips to the finals. On those occasions when I didn't get there I always got through to the Eastern Counties and the area finals, losing very few times over my career.

The second time I won it, in 1986, I beat the American Rick Ney in the final. If memory serves, I did drop a couple of legs that year but it's hardly surprising: you just think how many matches I had to play, especially in the Ilford area. We're there, on the corner of London and there were so many talented players in the competition. You start off playing at your local (I represented the King George V in Ilford when I first started but had moved to the Maypole in Hainault by 1986) and it was always the tradition that whoever got through from there, everyone else would go and support and follow that person for as far as they got.

More often than not it was me, and then it was on to somewhere like Barking for the regional round. There were literally hundreds of players still involved at that stage, all the individual winners from the pubs in that part of east London. It was like an open competition; the standard was so high. The first time I entered I couldn't believe how many people had got through, just from my area alone. Huge venues were needed just for the area finals and then for the next round and the round after that.

One year, Jocky was staying with me – he'd failed to qualify on that occasion but came along to support me at the area finals. He couldn't believe how many people were there and how many matches I had to play that day in order to get through to the grand finals. He told me that he'd only had to play about half that number when he'd qualified – and defeated me – a few years earlier. But this time, thanks in part to the wee fella cheering me on, I got through once again.

The history of darts has always fascinated me and when I look down the list of *News of the World* winners, I'm very proud to see my name twice '1979 R GEORGE' and '1986 B GEORGE', although anyone would probably think that two different Georges had won it!

I've always wondered how a chap called Johnny Bell must have felt. In both 1954 and 1955 he lost in the grand final. Imagine that, going through all those matches and getting to the final and losing. Then the following year he must have thought that it was his destiny to come back and win it but was again pipped at the post. Tom Reddington beat him in his second final, one of just seven players to have won the tournament twice. The first three were all called Tom – Tommy Gibbons and Tom Barrett the others – followed by Stefan Lord, Eric Bristow, me and Mike Gregory.

Unfortunately, you won't see any footage of my second win, in 1986, as it wasn't broadcast due to a technicians' strike that weekend. Sadly, the tournament had only a few more years to run before it was scrapped for good after the 1990 event, although Sky Sports did revive it for one year in 1997, providing Phil Taylor with the opportunity of getting his name on the honours board.

MY WORLD FALLS A-PART

EXCUSE ME for a moment whilst we have a further recap and this time it's some of the personal stuff, the stuff I'm most proud of and the stuff that helped shape my life.

During an event in London on 14 February 1984 I met Marie and there and then announced that I was going to marry her. And I did, three years later. Sons Robert and Richard duly arrived and our little family group was complete.

Apart from being the best wife, mother and grandmother anyone could wish for, Marie has always been there to support and encourage me in everything I've been involved in and practically runs the business side of things single-handedly. Without the help of Marie I'd have packed it all in years ago because I've neither the patience nor know-how to do what she does. She'll take the bookings, look up where the venues are, sort out the hotel and the routes and how long it will take to get there, then do the driving. She's business manager, company accountant, secretary and transport boss all in one, so from that side of things she's a diamond. Then she's got an 18-bedroom mansion to run as well as being there at every beck and call for Robert and Richard and their families.

By the time Marie and I got together I had been a regular inside the world's top half-dozen players and had lifted numerous titles as well as becoming a familiar face on television sets across the land. I became a born-again husband and dad and my focus was more on the lucrative exhibition circuit than on playing competitive darts, although I still had a burning ambition to win the Embassy and become World Champion.

In 1980 I'd had a good shot at it, coming close to beating Eric in the final, and I'd had other opportunities down the years but had failed to take them. Many were starting to believe that my chance had gone for good but in 1993 I was playing some of the best darts of my career and reached the semi-final, only to lose to Lowey in a match where I failed to make the most of my opportunities and missed doubles proved costly.

Darts was then engulfed in months of wrangling and by the time of the next Embassy, the big split had taken place with many players defecting to join the WDC (which eventually became the PDC). For those of us that remained committed to the BDO there was the little matter of trying to keep the Lakeside championships relevant and that was helped by having the usual committed coverage by the BBC.

In every sense the 1994 tournament was huge: to the organisation, to the broadcasters, to the sponsors, to the supporters and to the players that competed. Some exciting matches would help and so would a familiar face or two. That's perhaps why yours truly was chosen to open the event, playing the very first match live on New Year's Day. Neither myself, nor my Australian opponent Russell 'Rusty' Stewart, could see the board very well as the lighting was poor but it was the same for both of us and I took the match in three straight sets.

In the next round I only dropped one set in defeating Martin Phillips of Wales. Suddenly the draw was starting to open up for me and I strongly fancied my chances of beating Kevin Kenny in the quarters. He was one of the fastest throwers around and we rattled along in a good-humoured contest. It was pivotal that I clinched the second set to go 2-0 up because he was on a double, and I leapt high to celebrate as the dart found the double 4 bed.

As I landed, I felt a sharp pain in my back. Even Kevin heard it and asked if my back had gone, I was in constant excruciating pain for the remainder of the match and had to fight off a comeback from my opponent before somehow getting over the line. I hoped it was just a muscle spasm or something but deep down I knew it was so much worse than that and so it proved to be, with my leap of joy heralding the start of the most painful couple of days of my life.

Following a restless night, I headed straight to hospital the next morning and following my X-rays Dr Austin Brown looked straight at me and said, 'You can't play darts. You shouldn't even be able to walk. You've broken your back, Mr George.'

That should have been that, but of course, it wasn't. I was forthright in my belief that I could still get up on stage and compete and the fact that I knew I could beat my opponent, Sweden's Magnus Caris, made me all the more determined. It was foolhardy of me to even consider it, but I was so determined, knowing this might be my last chance to reach a world final.

They found me a steel corset and I was trussed up inside like a Christmas turkey about to go into the oven.

Trying to blank everything out as best I could, I found the focus and determination to roar into a 2-0 lead in a race to win five sets. Magnus was a decent enough player but if I continued at anything like the form I'd been showing then I knew that I'd be alright. But then the pain hit me again. Despite all the painkillers I'd taken just to get me on to the Lakeside stage, I knew inside that it was madness to think that I could continue to defy medical science and carry on playing. With all the distractions inside my mind, the match turned around quickly and I was left wondering how I'd let my lead slip and seen Magnus roar into a 4-2 advantage and have a dart at double 18 to take the place in the final that I so coveted.

Fortunately, he just clipped the outside of the wire and gave me a reprieve. I hit my double and was back in it. 'Fight, you tart,' I said to myself, by way of a pep-talk. The fans were magnificent, chanting for me throughout and gradually I fought my way back and scraped over the line with a winning double top.

I almost collapsed into the arms of MC Martin Fitzmaurice and somehow managed to hobble off stage and into the waiting arms of my Marie. What a state I was in. Every stitch of clothing was drenched with sweat and the pain was utterly unbearable.

The concern I now had was that I would have to go through it all again the following day for the final. Once more the doctors tried to talk me out of it and Marie didn't want me to play either but apart from my own health issues, I knew what it meant for the final to take place. The final of the BDO World Championship was always shown live on BBC television and brought huge viewing figures for the corporation, so they certainly weren't interested in the prospect of me pulling out.

Once word got around that I was struggling to compete I understand there were some suggestions that Magnus Caris should take my place in the final against Canada's John Part but what if he'd won? How could he claim to be World Champion when I'd beaten him in the semi-final? None of it made sense. The other option was for me to pull out and Part take the trophy and title on a walkover but the broadcasters weren't going to accept that without a huge fight.

What would be the repercussions for the BDO if they couldn't even stage their own world final? That shouldn't have been a concern for me at the time but it was and I decided to honour my obligations and take part, even though I knew that I would probably be well beaten.

The frustrating thing about that 1994 World Championship is that I was playing well enough to beat anyone before my injury and I think I would have beaten John Part in the final but for the extreme agony I was in. I'm told there was a goalkeeper who played in the FA Cup Final with a broken neck back in the day. If he was in anywhere near as much discomfort as me, then I feel for him because I was barely able to move due to the extreme pain.

There was all sorts of pressure – both external and internal – telling me to get up on that stage and play the final, even when the doctors were adamant that I shouldn't, under any circumstances. What could I do? I was a darts player and had battled through adversity to reach my second world final, knowing how disappointed I'd felt over losing the first one, 14 years earlier.

Foolishly, I suppose, I couldn't help but think it was my destiny to go on and lift the trophy at the second time of asking. After everything that had happened to me it almost seemed like the most unlikely outcome was about to happen.

John Part went on to have a brilliant career in top-level darts and became a three-time World Champion, collecting the PDC title in both 2003 and 2008 to add to his BDO one for beating me. In 1994 he was an unknown, unheralded player in this country and I know that had I been in good health I'd have beaten him, but it wasn't to be.

It was a poor final, statistically one of the worst, because I was outscoring him but couldn't twist or turn and throw at any of the doubles on either side of the board. John took his opportunity well, I can't blame him for that. He could only play what was in front of him and couldn't have had an easier night. Sid Waddell, on commentary, said that I looked like the Hunchback of Notre Dame but nothing else was really made of my condition and I was a little disappointed that John didn't at least acknowledge that I was far from being well in his victory speeches.

The crowd could see how much I was hurting though and continued to chant, 'Bobby, Bobby, Bobby' throughout the presentations. There and then I wished that I could have won it for them but my immediate priority soon turned to getting some surgery organised. After all, I'd just played in a World Championship final with a broken back!

SWINGS AND ROUNDABOUTS

A FOUR-HOUR operation to repair my back was only the start of a lengthy and expensive process to regain my fitness, but during the months of recuperation Marie and I spent a fair amount of time discussing our domestic arrangements. We'd been living in Halstead but had a burning desire to find somewhere with enough land to build our dream home and maybe some lakes where I could relax and fish as well. A mate of mine, Pat Long, knew what I was after and rang me one day to say that his wife, Vicky, had seen an advertisement for a plot of land in Ardleigh, Essex, which sounded perfect.

Pat was in the construction business and went and had a look for me. He had reservations but it sounded ideal, a project I could get my teeth into and build our forever-home.

Using the skills I'd learned in earlier life, I set about working night and day for 30 months, enlisting a little bit of help where necessary but basically doing most of the hard labour myself. I'd gone for gold when submitting my original plans to the council, having plans drawn up for a 28-bedroom mansion. Incredibly, everything was approved. I was so shocked that I decided to scale it down a little bit and re-submitted the plans with just 18 bedrooms. People ask me why I needed so many bedrooms in a domestic property. I tell them that it's because I like to make love to my wife in a different bedroom every night. I tell them that if she can find me, then she can make love to me. If she can't I'll be in Room 12!

When you build something, no matter how many rooms, then you tend to fill it up. If you build 18 bedrooms you fill them up, if I'd built 28 or 38 rooms, we'd have somehow filled them up.

Even after we'd moved in I still had lots and lots of jobs to do around the place and it was probably around six years after I'd bought the land and begun the massive undertaking of building the house that everything was pretty much how Marie and I had wanted it.

Whether George Hall would ever have become a reality if I hadn't broken my back is a fair question because the alternative would probably have been that I would have stayed healthy, won the 1994 BDO World Championship and barely had a minute to myself from that point forward. I couldn't have fitted in any more bookings if I had won it and certainly wouldn't have had enough spare time to build the house.

It's certainly turned out alright in the end, despite the excruciating pain I was in after my leap of joy against Kevin Kenny on the Lakeside stage. Swings and roundabouts, I suppose.

By the time that our new home had become habitable I was back working hard on my darts as well, playing and doing exhibitions all over the place, then back home doing the driveways and eventually digging out my long-cherished dream, my wonderful lakes.

When it came to naming the place, I was told that as I'd built it myself I could name it anything I wanted as long as there wasn't a place with the same name nearby, so Marie chose the name George Hall. We both liked it, even if one of the neighbours took a different view. One morning, when the sign had gone up, the local history teacher walked past and told me she was disgusted with me.

I asked her why and she said, 'George Hall? The Martells would turn in their graves. William the Conqueror lived on your land, right here. The nobleman Geoffrey de Mandeville also lived here and gave it to the Martell family as tenants.'

She certainly knew her history because the land had indeed had famous residents and visitors in the past. Even so, she needed telling.

'When I came here, darling,' I said, 'this was just a field. There was nothing on it, nothing at all, so I was going to call it "Fuck 'all" but the council wouldn't let me!'

FROM LAKESIDE TO LAKE SIDE

AS I'VE mentioned a time or two, I've always enjoyed fishing and always cherished an ambition to live somewhere with my own fishing lakes, so when I built George Hall that was in the back of my mind. Before we bought the land my mate Pat Long tested the ground. He dug down two feet and told me that it was blue clay, which is ideal for lakes. During my years of digging tunnels, I became very familiar with blue clay and knew that it breaks up like coal when it becomes semi-dry. For my needs, I knew it was the ideal substance to line the sides of the lake.

So, after building the house, we cracked on and dug out the lake and then waited for it to fill up with water. A few anxious days went by and then one morning, about a week later, Marie opened the curtains and was all excited. 'Come and look. Your dream has just come true,' she shouted.

I wasn't at my sharpest that morning, 'Dream, what do you mean? Has a parcel come or something?'

'No,' she said. 'The lake is there; you've got your own lake.'

The water had indeed risen and my hole in the ground had now become a lake. It was a lovely feeling to know that it had worked but there was no resting on any laurels and I set about building another lake. We already had a Roman pond there as well.

I hadn't ever intended it to be used as a fishery, it was just meant to be for my own pleasure but I wanted to do it all correctly and make sure it was safe to put the fish in. Firstly, I sought the proper advice before setting up the pumps, the aerators and some fountains. Then the plants were introduced before I began to get the fish established, again after carefully consulting people as to what I could have in there and what I couldn't.

Having let it all settle for a few weeks, I could see that everything was thriving and decided that it was time to get the rod out and have some 'me-time' but I needed a couple of pints of maggots first. Making my way down to the Colchester Bait and Tackle Shop, I went in to see if he'd got some and to see what other bait he might have.

'Where are you fishing then, Bob?' said the owner, a chap called Doug Titshall – who I became good friends with.

'Just in the back garden,' I told him, truthfully. From the look he gave me I think he thought I was a nutcase or something.

'Oh, you've got a pond in your garden,' he mused. 'Big, is it?'

'Well, I wouldn't like to drink it,' I laughed, before inviting him over to have a look for himself. Doug seemed impressed by my set-up and suggested that I put swims in and sell day tickets. We chatted about the possibility of opening it up for outsiders to use and realised it could be a nice little enterprise for us both. So, he sold my tickets alongside his bait and we took it from there and have hosted many matches and corporate days since then, plus all the casual day-ticket fishermen and friends that just want to come down and try their luck.

I'd like to think I've provided a bit of a service and do everything I can to make sure it remains healthy. You can't do too much in the winter but in the spring I get the environmental people in and they zap it for me and tell me how many fish are in the lakes and whether I need to re-stock that particular year or not. They're in the business and do it all the time so I take on board their recommendations and if they tell me there's a shortage of bream or carp or tench or whatever, I'll get some more.

It's important to do it properly because you can have too many, of course. That's when it doesn't become a sport; if the fish are starving hungry and there's so many of them you can't help but catch them. Some lakes just keep pouring fish in – I don't like that.

The pumps cost a lot of money to run. Most fisheries haven't got pumps but I've got the proper ones, plus the aerators and some massive fountains. To maintain it all isn't easy and I'm forever checking on the trees that surround the lakes. Fishermen can't fish properly if the trees are overhanging all around, so they regularly need cutting back. From time to time I'll take photographs and it's remarkable how branches can develop over such a short period of time.

But those lakes are my pride and joy and give me a lot of pleasure. They're hard work to maintain but I enjoy every minute of it.

INVITATIONS AND RED TAPE

LIFE IS a little easier for professional sportspeople if they are given a bit of a helping hand, especially when it comes to sponsors' invitations. Other sports have them: we've all heard the phrase used in tennis 'so-and-so has been given a wildcard for Wimbledon'. That's fine for the player getting the helping hand, unless your name is Bobby George.

My career has certainly benefitted from the tremendous support I've been given by my many sponsors. Durro were so good to me in the early stages, Courage Breweries became a reliable source of income for many years and the excellent relationship I always had with Winmau, the darts equipment manufacturers, has lasted for decades.

Key sponsors are essential and maybe due to my long-term association with Winmau and the fact that the Embassy World Championships wouldn't be the same without me, for a while I was often the beneficiary of a sponsor's invitation into the qualifiers of both the Winmau World Masters and the Embassy World Championships.

Obviously when I was at the peak of my career, my record in both events and my world ranking would guarantee me a spot in the main draw of both events. But once I'd had six years away from tournament darts, I had no recent record or rankings to fall back on. It wasn't just me that got a helping hand: former winners Leighton Rees, Eric, Jocky, plus a few others would get Embassy invitations after dropping down the rankings, but they would be put straight in to the main event, not the qualifiers.

Alan Glazier was another who was sponsored by Winmau and would always get a sponsor's invitation into the Masters, yet it was always me that everyone seemed to have an issue with. Folks used to give me stick saying I'd got an easy ride, a free passage into the tournament but that wasn't true; I only ever got sponsors' invitations into qualifying and everyone knows how hard it is to get through there.

Every year we had the same rigmarole over red tape because Olly Croft and the BDO always wanted signed letters from the sponsor before admitting me to the qualifiers, so it's amongst my proudest achievements to say that whenever I received an invitation I managed to get through to the main event.

The final occasion that I qualified for the Embassy was in 2002 when I gave Raymond van Barneveld a fair old run for his money before eventually bowing out of the competition for good with a ten-dart leg.

There have been frequent mentions of Olly Croft up to this point, so I should elaborate a little on how important he was to my career. Known to many as the 'Godfather of Darts', I simply called him God. Olly set up the BDO in 1973 and ran it until he was voted off the board in 2011. He and his wife Lorna – and an elected committee – pretty much handled everything during that period, setting up the inter-county structure and then the major events and the international competitions. They brought in sponsorship and broadcasting deals, so virtually every professional player that was involved at that time had cause to be grateful to Olly. Of course it wasn't easy for him, there were lots of spats and arguments and there were always claims that others could do a better job but darts would have been in a poorer state without Olly Croft.

One day he was pouring his heart out to me about the BDO's finances and saying that there was very little money coming in. I thought about it for a while and suggested he charge everyone £50 a year to become a member of the BDO. If you wanted to play in a BDO-organised event then you needed to pay the membership.

I've no idea how many people this would have involved but there were dozens of super-league teams up and down the land, with the majority of those players harbouring ambitions of furthering their careers at county level. Each would need to be a member before they could do so. I did some rough calculations and reckoned there might be as many as 10,000–15,000 members if this took off and the money would ease a bit of pressure on Olly and would mean there was some money in the kitty for production costs, hotels and that sort of thing.

He thought my idea was a non-starter but encouraged me to go to a county AGM. I went on stage and put my proposal to them, detailing all the benefits as I went along, even assuring them that they would effectively become shareholders.

The response was astonishing, to say the least.

'£50? We're not made of money,' said one.

'We can't afford that,' said some of them. 'We have to pay for our meals and drinks and petrol money, that sort of thing.'

'What about making it just £10 a year?' someone suggested.

I'd about had enough by then and told them so. '£10, that's around 20p a week. Are you hard up?

'You're pathetic,' I told them and walked out.

When Olly heard, he just said, 'I told you Bobby, they don't want to know. It's a waste of fucking time.'

Once Olly was voted out, that was the end of the BDO because things didn't work out for those that tried to follow him. Everything that the BDO had owned before was sold off or got rid of: stage settings, PA equipment, everything, it was all gone. And it was the end of the structure of darts in this country as we all knew it and the end of the BDO World Championships, which also meant the end of my BBC coverage.

A principled man, I felt for Olly, even though we'd had many run-ins over the years. He was incredibly saddened by the split, when many players defected to join the WDC in 1994.

THE CRAFTY TOMMY O

I'VE ALREADY told you how much I've enjoyed my visits to America over the years but generally that's because I've usually been over on the west coast. I have to reveal that I'm not really a fan of New York City at all. Tall buildings everywhere and it's freezing cold because the sun doesn't get on you and the wind is always whistling down the street. Every building seems to be an eating place; it's just not my cup of tea at all. So, it was with some reluctance that I accepted an invitation to go and do an exhibition tour there a few years ago, with Little Richard Ashdown by my side as my MC.

Part of the deal was that whilst I was there, I would present some trophies on behalf of the American Darts Organisation and answer some questions from the audience. They sent a car for us and we went and had a good time, as it happens. Then when it came to the audience participation, two old boys stood up.

'Bobby,' said one of them. 'Do you remember us?'

I looked at them for some sort of clue but it was pointless. 'Give over,' I answered. 'I don't remember what I had for breakfast. Who are you?'

This fella said, 'We played in the 1980 North American Open Pairs.'

'Did you?' I asked, starting to get interested.

He went on. 'We sure did man, we sure did. We both come from New York City and we saved up for more than a year to go to Los Angeles to play in that tournament.' In Great Britain we tend to forget that it's almost as far to get from New York to LA as it is to go from New York to London, so fair play to them. But he then went on to tell a darting story that must be unique.

'My mate here was a good shooter,' he confirmed. 'I wasn't a bad scorer, but he was a good shooter,' he said. That's what they tended to call them over there, 'shooters!'

He went on, 'We practised for a year in my den. Three times a week my mate came round, and we played darts, legs of 301 double in double out, the same as they play in the tournament. So, we entered the pairs and made the trip over. First round we were the first names pulled out ... we were drawn to play against Bobby George and Tony Sontag from England.'

Now that year it was not only 301, double in and double out, but they'd also brought in that you had to throw for the bull before each leg. So, in a sense the luck is taken out of things, it's down to your ability. You need to win the bull to throw first and you need to get that double to get off.

This bloke had clearly told the story a few times over the years as he recited it all so perfectly. 'I remember you went up and hit the 25 and my mate missed.

'You went off 160 – double top, treble 20, treble 20. My mate couldn't get a double in any of his three darts, so we were in trouble. Tony then went up and hit 60 – 45 – 36 game shot. The perfect game.

'Second leg, you won the middle again and once more started with 160.

'My mate missed the doubles and Tony finished with 141 once more. We'd saved all our god darn money up to go to the North American Open and … do you know what title I hold …?

He paused for comic effect because he'd got the rest of the audience captivated by this stage.

'I'm the only person to ever enter the North American Open pairs, play a match and not throw a single dart!'

The room was in fits of laughter; he'd recited the story well and clearly has had a few laughs from it over the years. I couldn't remember if all of his details were correct or not, it's so long ago, but I know we did throw a few perfect legs from time to time and I do know that Tony and I went on to win it that year. No one could get anywhere near us.

I do remember coming up against a familiar face on our way to that final. The great Tommy O'Regan was there. He'd won the National Singles twice and was quite a player but he'd also been my mentor when I'd first started playing. What a character Tommy was, the only darts player to have played for and captained two different countries. When England played for the first time he was selected as captain and then when Ireland began playing international matches, he was made their captain as well.

Over the years he'd learned a few tricks of the trade, shall we say, and was keen to pass many of them on to his young protégé. I told this story in my first book but that was so long ago I assume most of you will have forgotten it – and in any case, if a story was worth telling 20 years ago, it sure as hell is worth another go now.

I'd only just started playing but he knew I'd got a bit of something about me and was always keen to further my darting education. He told me that he'd got an exhibition at Chigwell Police Headquarters and felt it would be good experience for me to go along with him and see how it went. No one could get anywhere near him. Then it came to the part of the evening when he'd do one of his party-pieces, something he'd become quite notorious for.

He asked if there was anyone in the audience who smoked and then invited a volunteer to come up on to the stage. His trick was to get someone with a cigarette in their mouth, position them accurately in front of the board, then throw a dart that would knock the fag out of his mouth and pin it to the double 10.

This big burly copper lit his cigarette and stood there ready, but it was nothing more than a dog-end he was smoking really. Tommy asked him if he'd got another cigarette but the bloke said it was his last one.

'Oh, that will do, then, we'll have a go,' said Tommy.

The policeman was very nervous and began to wobble a little bit. I was sat there watching. Taking it all in. Now I'd seen Tommy do this trick many times and never seen it go wrong but on this particular night he threw the dart straight into the bloke's nose.

Fucking hell!

Straight into his hooter it went … it was wobbling about with a dart embedded in it.

'Brandy quick!' shouted Tommy. 'Bring a brandy.'

The bloke took the dart out of his nose. The brandy came, Tommy dipped his finger in the brandy, rubbed it on the wound and then drank the rest of the brandy himself.

Everyone was in uproar; except the poor bloke he'd hit.

I thought 'you crafty so and so …' He was so clever; he'd made fun out of a situation that shouldn't have happened and got a glass of brandy out of it.

Around this time Tommy was living in Walthamstow, not too far from me, and I used to play money races with him. He was well known for his darting prowess and always looking for someone who thought they might be able to beat him for money.

'Anyone want to play the great Tommy O'Regan?' he'd bellow.

If there were no takers he'd put me on the spot.

'Or if you won't play me, do you reckon you could beat the big fella?' That was me.

He always wanted to play for money and was always hustling. 'You got £50 on you, just in case we lose?' he'd whisper.

He'd agree on the terms, one leg of 3,001 for £50 and then he'd take the chalks. In the days before digital or electronic scoreboards, everything was done with a board and chalk. Tommy was so crafty. We'd be involved in the game and then when he got to the bottom of the board he'd quickly wipe off all the scores and put fresh ones back on the top, carefully taking an extra 100 off my total and adding an extra 100 to my opponent's.

I'd think, 'What's going on here …? This was close a minute ago, now I'm well in front.' No one ever twigged … even if the poor bloke was playing well against me he was getting further behind, thanks to the crafty Mr O'Regan.

Then I'd win and he'd say 'well done, here's your money', and he'd give me a tenner and pocket the rest. If I ever lost, which was rare over that distance, he'd expect me to stump up the full £50 myself.

Darts was still quite a new way for me to spend my evenings and going out and about with Tommy accelerated my education. They were mainly good times, we'd make some money and have a few laughs, but it gave me that added bit of pressure to contend with and got me used to playing against all-comers and knowing there was a bit at stake.

Tommy knew all the tricks but he couldn't throw anywhere near as well from the 8ft mark. The regulation pub throw in those days was from 7ft 6in, with the occasional major tournament, especially the *News of the World* Championship, pushing the players back a further 6in. Nowadays the throw has been standardised to 7ft 9.25in. The modern players can pound the treble 20 with ease and occasionally folks will ask me if the oche should be pushed back to 8ft again. I don't think they'll ever do it but I do wish they'd put the size of the trebles back to how they were; they're far too big these days.

It's great technique to keep hitting 180s and 140s all night, don't get me wrong – but you practically need a goalkeeper in there nowadays. Maybe a goalkeeper with a shield. If you compare a new board with one of the older ones, you'll see a massive difference in the size of the trebles. Some folks will say, 'It's the wires Bobby, the wires are thinner.' It's nothing to do with the wires, the trebles are so much larger, so it's how much space is between the wires that counts.

There are also far fewer bounce-outs nowadays but I tell them I wasn't there to hit the wires, I was there to hit what's between them.

Of course, it's a great skill to aim for the wire and hit it. I regularly do exhibitions with Martin 'Wolfie' Adams, who's a lovely fella but I can occasionally pull the wool over his eyes. The former captain of England, the three-time BDO World Champion was watching me practise somewhere on an old-fashioned board and I hit the wire on the corner of the treble 20 bed and the dart bounced out.

'Hit the wire then, Bobby?' he said.

'Yes mate,' I responded. 'Aimed for it and hit it. Playing well, aren't I?'

'Really?' he exclaimed. 'You aimed for the wire?'

'Yes,' I said. Of course, I wasn't aiming for the wire but I told him that I had been. On his next throw he hit the wire and also had a bounce-out. He turned to me and had the cheek to claim that he'd thrown for it deliberately.

'I'm also playing well Bobby, aren't I?'

PICK A CARD, ANY CARD

THERE WERE occasions when I threw for the wire deliberately and when I also had other difficult challenges. Out on the exhibition circuit with Little Richard Ashdown as my MC, I'd do all sorts of speciality shots to liven up an evening and give the audience something different to enjoy, rather than just leg after leg of 501 or 301.

We'd have a series of cards lying face down on the table, with the name of a game written on the underside of each one. When a player came up to challenge me, they would pick one. Pick a card, any card and that's the game we'd play.

One game was called Bulls Hit (there may or may not be a gap between the S and the H!). The challenger had to play the normal 501 down whilst I could only score on 25s or bullseyes. The only way I could finish from 301 or 501 would be to leave 26 and go out on double 13.

For Shanghai Surprise, I had to hit the treble, single and double of any nominated number before my opponent finished from 301.

There was one particular night when I played a Welsh bloke, Mark Salmon I think his name was, and folks had said he could play a bit. He turned over the Shanghai Surprise card and my MC that night was Paul 'Slapper' Taylor, who asked him which number he wanted me to go for. Without hesitation he chose 5. 'Righto,' I said. 'Off you go.'

'Nah, you go first,' he replied, all cocky, clearly fancying his chances against me. I told him that he should throw first but he insisted. So, I went to the board and popped in a single 5, treble 5 and double 5, thank you. Game over. I'd hit the nominated Shanghai number and beaten him before he'd even had a shot and to great amusement from the crowd Slapper rubbed it in by announcing, 'Mark, your average is zero.'

This bloke wasn't amused and did his nut. I thought he was going to start a punch-up, so I told him to calm down.

'That's the fun of the game mate, you should have gone first. Tell you what, let's do it again. You can have one more chance. Pick me a number.'

He said, 'Five again.'

I told him to pick something different but he told me that I wouldn't hit it twice in a row.

'Go on then, off you go,' I told him but he again insisted I should have first throw. I went single, treble, double. Game over again. Now fuck off.

Again, he'd not thrown a dart. From his demeanour I thought he was going to kill Slapper but common sense prevailed and he stormed off.

For the game we called Bobby George I had to hit a nominated double for each of the six different letters in my name. B-O-Y-G-E-R. Little Richard would ask my opponent to nominate a double: usually 1, 3 or 17 were chosen first, and I'd pin the double and he'd cross the letters out.

On a good night I'd win the leg in just two visits! Sometimes I'd give the punter the choice of me throwing for the letters in his (or her) name instead. That stopped after the night I played an Indian gentleman who had 20 different letters in his full name. True story!

One of the hardest games I played on an exhibition night was called Three Different Colours. I had to come down from 501 but had to hit three different colours on the board for my score to count. So, I might throw one dart into a red segment, one into a black and one in a green, for example.

That one is really hard to do and I'd tell Little Richard not to give me that early on in the evening, let me get into it all first.

More often than not I'd be using my own stage gear and board set-up, so it would always be the same throw for me but I always liked to ease my way into an exhibition, improving as I went along and peaking towards the end. Always finish by leaving a good impression if you can.

Hitting three different colours each time was tricky but it was made a little bit easier by having Little Richard with me. He was so quick with the figures. If I had, say, 101 left, he'd quickly tell me to go for treble 15 (a green segment), single 16 (white) and double top (red).

We worked out that the least you can do that particular game in is just 11 darts and I did it a few times. I reckon that is harder than a conventional nine-darter. With Little Richard being as fast as he was, I was able to get into a rhythm and just hit whatever he called.

'Big black 10,' he'd say and boom, I'd hit it.

'Green treble 11,' boom, and so on.

I doubt I could have done it with anyone else Little Richard is so good with the numbers he'd always have a couple of different combinations up his sleeve as I neared a finish. Very clever and the audience generally realised the amount of skill that was involved from both of us. When that one went well it gave us both a great deal of satisfaction.

For the Barrymore Shot, my opponent had to tell me which part of the double I had to hit, top, middle or bottom. We played as normal but once we'd got to the double – say double 18 – they were asked to tell me exactly which part of the bed I had to check out on. That sometimes caused a few arguments but more often than not I'd pin exactly where I'd been challenged to hit.

There was another one where I had to finish on anything that my opponent chose. And by that, I mean anything. I might get down to a double and Little Richard would tell the player that they could nominate something different for me if they wanted and they'd usually opt for something simple, like double one. Little Richard would then steer the player towards some of the writing on the outside of the board and they'd eventually twig on and ask me to hit a particular letter or one of the numbers.

If it was a lady playing, he'd suggest one of the rings on the number 8. He'd have his little sayings to entertain the crowd, who always loved that sort of stuff. 'Would you like it in the big hole or the small hole, madam?'

If I hit the larger ring on the 8 he'd then go, 'Would you now like Bobby to slip it into the small one?'

You know you are playing well when you can hit targets of that size at will but most nights I would do it without any bother at all and the audience would be generous with their applause. Most of them knew their darts and knew how difficult some of our routines were to execute.

There were days when I was playing in exhibitions and I never missed a thing, nothing. I hit absolutely everything I threw for over a couple of hours and I used to think if ever I had days like that in the big events I'd have cleaned up and won far more than I did.

I really enjoyed the challenge of doing different things on a dartboard, just seeing how creative I could be and how entertaining that would be for those watching. Playing legs of 501 repeatedly is boring, I found. Little Richard helped me devise some of those games and we could guarantee there would be lots of giggles every night. I was the first darts player to put on a proper evening of entertainment when we were booked for an exhibition. They were always great fun to do, both for Little Richard and myself but most importantly for the punters, the guys and gals that had paid to come along and be entertained.

Not everyone saw that at first, of course. One night we were booked to do a show in a pub in Bristol. Great big place it was, with a long corridor that had cabinets stuffed full of darts trophies all the way down it.

We began to set our things up and then the landlord came and immediately knocked us off our stride.

'I don't want any of your Mickey Mouse games tonight,' he said, almost sneering with contempt. 'I've got the best players in the area here tonight ready to take you on. You show me if you're as good as you think you are.'

Roly Bright was with me that night as my MC. Ex-chairman of Suffolk darts, he knew his stuff and raised an eyebrow towards me.

'Military tonight then, Bob.'

That meant we were going to be on it. No fooling around, no messing, just solid, no-nonsense darts.

If that's what they wanted, then that's what they were going to get.

When you're put in that sort of situation then it's almost no-win. You're expected to beat the local pub players and never hear the end of it if you don't, so you just think, 'Please let me play my normal game and have a good night. Don't let me down.' On that particular night I didn't want to lose to any of them and didn't.

I played 15 or so matches of 501 and I thrashed them all.

Roly was loving it, calling out the 140s and the 180s … 'Game shot, and the next player is …'

Inside one hour and 20 minutes I'd stuffed the lot of them and went up to the bar to have a drink.

The landlord said, 'Bloody hell, I'll admit I didn't think you were that good.'

'Really?' I said. 'What do you mean?'

'I just didn't think you'd beat all of them like that, they're the best players in the area.'

'Unbelievable,' I thought. But I told him that it wasn't an exhibition, all I was doing was just a repetition of a game: 501, game shot, next.

As luck would have it, I was due to be just up the road the following evening and knew it would be a different sort of evening.

I told him to come along, 'Get in your car, come and see us tomorrow night and see what you think.' I hoped he would take me up on the offer but nevertheless, I was a little surprised to see him there in the audience, but he got the full experience as we put on our normal show, all the cards, some brilliant darts and plenty of fun and laughter along the way. Everyone had a top night, including my landlord pal and he came over afterwards and said he was man enough to admit he'd had a change of heart.

'What a fucking idiot I was, that was proper entertainment,' he said. He'd built his players up to try to beat me – fair enough – but if you're charging people on the door for a night's entertainment then I prefer it if they get the full package. If people leave and haven't had a good time then I haven't done my job. I want them to be entertained and if I do that, then I've almost certainly enjoyed it as well.

Another game we played with the cards was called The Stalker. The challenger would go first and whatever score they got I'd try to match it. So, if they hit 26 I'd try to get 26, but maybe choosing to do it in a different way. We'd play like this all the way down until I was in range and then I'd try and sneak in and finish before they could.

It was funny to watch as I matched their score each time but there was always pressure on me hitting whatever they scored. Occasionally someone would hit a 180 and on my good days I'd then hit one of my own in response and the place would go potty.

Everyone enjoyed that and of course I never knew what they were going to hit. Hitting 180s is the highlight of the night for some people and one night I was doing an exhibition in Tottenham for a firm that sold peanuts. I had to double-check that one and make sure they paid in cash! About halfway through the evening I'd not managed to hit a single 180. One of their reps mentioned it and I had to agree with him that I hadn't. He said, 'Play me one leg of 501 and for every 180 you hit I'll donate £180 for a local charity.'

I started off by hitting 180, 180 and he called me a c**t and every other nasty thing in the world. 'You set me up, you bastard,' he wailed. I promised him that I hadn't, that's just how it goes sometimes.

During the time that Little Richard was with me we managed to bounce off each other well. He had all the patter in the world and it all became a bit of a routine; we made it look pretty slick most of the time. When I went to an event with him, we took along a leprechaun puppet – you know the sort of thing, one that I could put on my knee and work from the inside with my hand. The leprechaun was a belter, kitted out in green felt, big hat, ginger beard, the works. I'd then try to be a ventriloquist and move his head and mouth, as I tried to throw my voice.

'Gockle of geer.'

Ken Dodd used to do it with his Diddymen, only I think he did it a bit better than me!

At the end of the evening, time permitting, I would take some questions from the audience and I'd often get asked how I met Little Richard.

I'd be holding the puppet and would tell a story of how I had been travelling through Ireland and had stumbled upon a leprechaun sitting on a pot of gold.

The leprechaun said, 'Top of the morning to you Bobby, do you want some gold?'

I said, 'No thank you, I have plenty of gold.'

The leprechaun then said, 'For not taking the gold I will grant you two wishes.'

I thought about it for a moment and said, 'Then I'd like a 5ft dick with a good head.

'And that, ladies and gentlemen, is when he gave me Richard Ashdown!'

That always got a few laughs; we had many a giggle with that puppet. It was just something different to add on an exhibition night, something the punters clearly weren't expecting. I don't imagine it's something you'd see anywhere today as many of the players that I see are just out to bash the punters up as quickly as they can.

As a night out, that becomes pretty boring and not particularly entertaining. I get that it's a great thrill to play and test yourself against any of the top professionals and see how you get on against them, but in terms of a show I always thought about the humorous side of darts and was always looking to come up with ways to entertain, whilst also being tested on the board myself.

Incidentally, mighty oaks come from small acorns but Little Richard Ashdown will never get any taller. Despite that, his own career has blossomed 'skywards' and I couldn't be prouder of him.

He has always been able to count quicker than a calculator and jumped at the opportunity to become a 'spotter' for televised darts after I recommended him to the BBC in 2002.

Since then, he's worked for all the major broadcasters both in front of and behind the cameras and for several years took over at the Lakeside as the MC for the BDO World Championships.

Whilst we still catch up regularly and occasionally do stuff together, in recent times I've worked a lot with Paul Booth, another excellent MC who is a regular face as the ring announcer at many of the large, televised boxing events. Extremely professional, his stage attire is spot on, always with the black suit, bow tie and patent shoes. He looks the business and I call him the 'James Bond of Darts'. He likes that!

Paul is a one-man band, who puts the stage up, does the scoring, plays the music and calls the games. For me, Paul and his equipment are the best in the business.

Having a few laughs has always been a major part of my exhibitions and that fits in nicely with the way Paul goes about his business as well. He gets me and what I'm trying to deliver to the audience but I'm never sure what he's going to come up with when he introduces the punters on to the stage to play me. He has a few favourite lines, which always have the house in stitches.

As you'll have noticed I've worked with quite a lot of excellent MCs over the years but it's perhaps fair to say that not many are as saucy as Paul, and that's saying something because I once used to work with Roy 'Chubby' Brown. Paul also used to be Eric Bristow's MC and was there on that very sad evening in 2018 when my mate passed away.

Two other excellent guys I've worked with over the years are Paul Hinks and John McDonald. Paul is what I regard as an old-fashioned caller and I call him 'Mr 45' because there's no finer sound in darts than Paul calling out 45 in his own distinctive style – I used to hit it deliberately sometimes in exhibitions, just to hear him call it.

John is perhaps best known for being the master of ceremonies at most of the big PDC televised tournaments. Once we spent a few days working together in Ireland, with John doing all the driving and generally looking after me. One day I fell ill and we had to cancel the booking for that evening. I was so poorly that Jason Thame, who runs MODUS, the company that had organised the tour, brought me a load of shirts and other bits and bobs for me to sign, as he was worried in case I pegged it!

Thanks to John I was soon back on my feet and since then I have called him the nurse.

KNIVES AND NAILS

WITHOUT TRYING to manufacture a connection between your local darts league and a primitive caveman, it has always been a basic human requirement to be able to project a missile and try to hit a target. If a caveman was a good hunter, then his family would get the very best meat for their dinner; those not-so-accurate spear-chuckers had to make do with the berries.

Some of us have an excellent eye and some not so good, so although I'd known nothing about darts until that fishing trip, I'd always somehow known I had an ability to throw things and see them land in the designated target.

Back when I was a kid, you'd occasionally see a knife-throwing act on one of the television variety shows. You know the drill, a shiny-suited geezer would build up the drama by sharpening his blades and popping a couple of balloons. Then his glamorous assistant would have her arms and legs strapped to a spinning wheel and slowly be rotated. We all feared for her life as he threw a couple of knives that appeared to be perilously close to her. As the act built towards a crescendo he'd pop on a blindfold and somehow manage to fling those deadly weapons to within a couple of inches of her spinning form.

You'll have read in my first book, I hope, that academically I wasn't the most gifted in my year at school but I was good with my hands and once the metalwork teacher had shown me the rudiments of the subject there was no stopping me. I knew exactly what I wanted to make: my own set of throwing knives. I'm not sure the teachers would turn a blind eye to a pupil doing that these days but it was a different era and anyone who showed a glimmer of enthusiasm for a subject was given every encouragement.

Across a couple of lessons, I made and sharpened my knives and took them home to practise with and learn how to throw them properly. From a distance of about 20ft I became quite proficient and it's a difficult skill to master, because you have to throw them quite hard for them to reach the target and stick in. I would stand there for hours, throwing my knives until I became quite good at it.

There was no grand plan about it, I wasn't about to go around boasting how good I was at throwing a knife at a bit of timber, but it did give me a slight sense of achievement. This was something I'd taught myself to do, however insignificant it may seem to others. When you see people in the films, they throw the knife holding the blade but the knife should be thrown by the handle otherwise you cut your hands on the blade: it's not easy.

It wasn't just the knives, because I loved throwing anything I could get my hands on and was also pretty good with a bow and arrow. They used to call me Robin Hood whenever I was out with my bow, which was quite ironic because I learned that

I was actually going to be called Robin as a baby but they wrote down and registered me as Robert, although my dad continued to call me Robin for many years.

Even though darts didn't come into my life until I was 30, there must have been something there, surely? Isn't it funny how you can have a particular skill without knowing that you've got one. I suppose it's all down to hand/eye co-ordination: some people have it, some don't.

Later on, when I first started doing my darts exhibitions, I would always look at different ways to entertain and knew that some players had become proficient at throwing 6in nails into a dartboard. I practised and practised that skill and eventually became good enough to introduce it into my routines. Ensuring that the nails are as sharp as you can get them is paramount and then you've got to get the distance right to get the gravity pull on the nail but once you do that it's something that I found quite easy to master. One, two, three spins before it hits the board. Four spins if you stand a little further back.

It generates quite a bit of interest when an audience sees it for the first time but I found that it can muck your darts up if you do it too much. It was alright to do it as a gimmick but I had to make my name as a darts player first and quickly realised that the only way to do that was to learn my craft the hard way.

Whilst I've mentioned many of the different card-type games I used in my exhibitions, there was still time for some favourite old-fashioned trick shots. One of the most famous examples of that came when I appeared on the *Rod Hull and Emu Show*. Rod was famous for creating mayhem and havoc by using his Emu puppet to grapple playfully with his guests. He could get away with anything with Emu on his arm and it was all great fun as we fooled around on the sofa.

Then we moved to the dartboard where Emu, after much persuasion from Rod, was positioned in front of the bullseye. Pretending to be nervous throughout the trick shot, Emu quivered anxiously as I fired half a dozen darts all around its beak before finally firing one towards the bull, which found its target as Rod expertly opened the puppet's mouth at exactly the right moment. It was a great bit of theatre, a throwback to the old music hall acts, with Emu standing in as my glamorous assistant.

ENGELBERT

WHEN I pause to think of some of the remarkable things I've done and some of the incredible people I've met, I guess singing on stage in Las Vegas with Leo Sayer would be right up there, as would meeting Diana Ross on the same trip, although she didn't have a clue who I was.

Those experiences were mentioned in *Bobby Dazzler* but since then I've got to know another famous musician quite well: the one and only Engelbert Humperdinck. Enge, to his friends, knew Bob Potter through work. Bob, you will probably know, owned a couple of leisure complexes, including the Lakeside Country Club at Frimley Green, where the BDO World Championships found a home. Most of the world's top musicians, comedians and variety acts have performed at the Lakeside over the years, including Enge. Unbeknown to almost everyone, the singer turned out to be a massive darts fan and apparently yours truly was one of his favourite players. Chatting to Bob, Enge revealed that he'd love the chance to play a couple of legs with me.

The wheels were set in motion, Bob gave me a call and I was happy for the singer to pop by George Hall when he was next in the area. Somehow the BBC got wind of it and asked if they could film it, hoping it would make a nice little piece to run during the next World Championships.

We had a great time and he was no mug on the dartboard, certainly one of the best celebrity opponents I've faced. The Beeb turned it into a nice piece, with the feature starting with a shot of me on our stairs, singing 'Please release me, let me go' (which I think would be a great song for any player suffering with dartitis). Obviously I was miming, with the great man singing his biggest hit off camera.

Enge was only going to stop for an hour or so but ended up staying all day, all evening and well into the night, whilst we played, chatted, drank and ate. It was lovely to spend time with a star performer, someone who had probably appeared on every stage in the world and alongside all of the biggest names in show business.

When he'd first gone to America he'd hooked up with Elvis Presley and the pair became good mates. Engelbert's trademark look was the long, dark sideburns and he says that the most famous performer of his generation asked him if it would be OK if he grew some like it.

A lot of his stories centred upon Hollywood and the stars of that area. He told me that he'd bought Jayne Mansfield's house there – a luxury mansion called the Pink Palace – but when he moved in it absolutely stank. It turned out that she'd kept lions or tigers or something and the smell of the big cats' urine lingered around a lot longer than she had. His first job was to rip out all the floorboards and start again.

Enge's only frustration was that he left George Hall without a win – and boy did he try. He threw some really good darts against me but I wasn't about to let him win just for the sake of it, even though he mentioned that he'd managed to beat Phil Taylor and Eric Bristow when he'd played against them in the past.

At one point during the filming, Marie put some music on, Tom Jones singing 'It's Not Unusual'. We thought it would wind him up but he wanted it left on, admitting he was a big fan of the Welsh crooner and that was one of his favourite songs.

When the BBC ran the feature it ended with shots of Engelbert throwing and hitting a 180 – I wonder who actually threw those darts?

Later, when my two boys returned home, he asked if he could play them. Richard gave him a right old bashing, Enge couldn't get anywhere near him. 'He can play, can't he?' whispered our guest.

'Do you play as well?' he asked Robert, who has always been a bit of a dark horse when it comes to darts but on his day is a really good player. Again, Engelbert couldn't win a leg. He was getting a bit exasperated, so I asked if he wanted to play Marie next!

'No, no more, I'm done,' he said. Then we sat and talked until he remembered that his driver had been sat outside in the car all day! When he brought this fella in, it turned out to be someone that I'd played with in the super league all those years ago when I first started. It's a small world.

Engelbert invited Marie and myself to one of his shows, where we went backstage and had a further catch-up with him and his family.

Someone I met from a different walk of life was the Brazilian footballer Sandro. He played for Spurs between 2010 and 2014 and had got into the darts by watching on television and then playing with his team-mates at the club's training ground. I was introduced to Sandro by a mutual friend and we enjoyed an afternoon at George Hall which was filmed for football's *Premier League Show*. They made it into a rather amusing little feature, where both my son Richard and I played a few legs with the samba star.

We all got on so well that we accepted an invitation for a return match back at Sandro's. He was quite a funny lad but his English wasn't up to much, so I taught him a few choice phrases and soon had him saying 'lovely jubbly' at random moments.

The first thing I had to do was re-set his dartboard because he'd got it far too low and hadn't even got a proper mark for the oche, so we sorted all that and then had a few legs. Afterwards, we had a couple of beers together and his mum cooked some food for us all, before Sandro brought out his guitar and started singing for us. Richard accompanied him on the tambourine and then they swapped over and I discovered that my son could play the guitar really well!

'How did you learn to do that so quickly?' I asked him.

'I just watched which chords he used and copied him,' replied Richard.

Sandro told us that he was always fearful of being robbed and made sure that he sent his money back to Brazil for his family. He and Richard saw each other a few times after that, before he was transferred abroad.

The BBC ran a feature called 'A Leg With Bobby', which was always a very popular segment during the Lakeside event and I never knew who they were going to bring along to play against me. It was generally a very simple format, as the title suggests. A game of darts and a quick chat, usually done between the afternoon and evening sessions of play.

Eric always used to ask me how I seemed to do it so effortlessly, which I took as a compliment because there was a bit of pressure on me to keep the chat interesting and to chuck some decent darts as well. There was no point me bashing in steady tons or whatever if the guest had barely thrown a dart in his life, so in those instances I'd try and pull out a few trick shots, three double 10s or something.

It was a bit of fun and went down well with the viewers, who were obviously keen to see me come a cropper. Often, I'd be playing against one of the leading politicians of the day but a couple of the most memorable encounters were with comedian Jim Davidson and the snooker player Mark Selby. I don't think Jim actually got round to throwing any darts, he just kept us in stitches with some of his gags, whereas Selby showed that he isn't just a talent on the green baize but is also a terrific darts player.

LEAGUE OF LEGENDS

THERE IS always a clamour from people to relive our youth. We're all the same, we like to be reminded of things that made us happy when we were younger. That's why bands are always getting back together to try to rekindle the 'good old days' when they were hugely successful.

Darts is no different: for years people suggested that some of us oldies should have tournaments just for ourselves. They wanted to see Bristow, Lowe, Jocky and myself going toe-to-toe once again.

Nowadays there is a chance for those that reach the age of 50 to compete on their own tour: the World Seniors Darts is professionally organised and run and, thanks to television coverage, it is growing year upon year.

Back in 2008 that was all a pipe dream but the first steps to its formation came when Setanta Sports agreed to screen the League of Legends, a darts tournament for the more elderly participant, shall we call it. It was the idea of Lee Henderson, a sports promoter from the north-east, who said that he'd get the sponsorship and the television coverage and cover the prize money and, bless him, he did.

The sports bookmaker BetFred came on board straight away and agreed to sponsor the event, so all that needed doing was to confirm the eight players who would feature.

Bristow, Lowe and myself were involved from the start and were asked for our opinions on who should join us. Bearing in mind that some of the sport's legendary names were no longer with us, the list was whittled down quite easily to former World Champions Bob Anderson and Keith Deller, plus Cliff Lazarenko and Dave Whitcombe. That made up seven of the eight places but we disagreed strongly on who should complete the line-up. I felt it should be Mike Gregory, whose record stacked up against anybody: he'd reached a BDO world final, lost in two Masters finals and emulated my record of winning the *News of the World* crown, not once but twice.

I was shocked when Eric and co said they were against it being Mike. 'Why?' I was confused.

They put forth an argument that Mike had been part of the breakaway group that joined the WDC, prior to the formation of the PDC. Even though he later backtracked and came back to the BDO, he had twice won the Lada UK Masters during the split, winning a car each time. They called him a Judas.

'It was only a fucking Lada,' I pointed out. It wasn't as if it was a Rolls-Royce. They may have improved in quality over the years, but when he won his two Ladas, they were Ladas!

Poor Mike was outnumbered and so was I. They went for Peter Evison, a winner of the World Masters and World Matchplay, to make up our eight and although I thought it was the wrong choice, the meeting was over.

Incidentally, I went into a shop the other day and asked if they'd got a window wiper for a Lada. The bloke behind the counter said, 'That sounds like a fair swap!'

The League of Legends was hugely successful, televised live over eight consecutive Fridays, with opening night and finals night being staged at the iconic Circus Tavern. In between we travelled the country, playing at Birmingham, Blackburn, Batley, Stoke, Reading and Bridlington. Sold-out venues gave us the very best support imaginable and the fans weren't shy in letting us know how much they were enjoying seeing us in competitive action all over again. It also gave a new audience, both in the venues and watching at home on TV, a chance to enjoy the Bobby George walk-on for the first time.

My only disappointment was that I didn't play well enough to reach the final that year; Anderson beat Deller in case you're interested. In terms of prize money, it didn't matter as we'd all agreed to split everything eight ways from the start.

That was something I had to remind Keith of a year later. The initial tournament had gone so well that it was an automatic decision to do it again in 2009. All the venues were good to go and the tickets were snapped up but then we were hit by the news that Setanta had gone bust and there went our television coverage. We still fulfilled our obligations and went ahead with series two and I found a bit of form and reached the final against Deller. I'm still not sure what he was up to that night but he suddenly went all arsey and started barracking me and taking it all very seriously.

I said, 'What are you doing?' and had to remind him that there was no extra prize money for winning; it was a Mickey Mouse cup in reality and I told him he could have it if he wanted it that badly. The crowd booed him something rotten and he came over and apologised. 'I didn't mean it, Bobby.'

It soured the event a little bit for me, bloody chalk flying all over the place as well. Generally, Keith and I rub along just fine but on some occasions I've not quite understood where he's coming from. But, as Eric always used to say, 'Just ignore them all, Bob; we don't have to like people to work with them!'

The League of Legends had shown that there were enough folks out there who were interested in what some of us old darts players had to offer, so in 2009 the idea was floated for some of us to do a theatre tour of Great Britain. Eric, John Lowe and myself were booked in to play around 40 dates as 'Legends of the Oche', hosted by the very funny comedian Duncan Norvelle.

We were all looking forward to it but then I had to have surgery after doing my arm in. I'd somehow broken my collarbone and damaged my rotator cuff and was in great discomfort for a while. I told them that regrettably I'd have to pull out of it but Lowey was insistent that I came along as arranged. 'You're a good talker Bob, you do that bit and me and Eric will do the darts.'

So, whilst I was getting better, that's what happened. Eric would play a few punters and then do an interview with Duncan, Lowey would do his bit and then I'd do the full walk-on with the music and cloak and everything and do a question and answer session.

We all had a laugh right at the start of the tour because the very first player to come on stage beat Eric in just 12 darts.

'Fucking hell, where'd you get him from?' wailed the Crafty Cockney. 'I'd have needed a nine-darter to beat him,' which was true.

Duncan was excellent, he'd get things going with his own comedy set and would throw in plenty of gags throughout. He knew his darts as well; in fact he wasn't a bad player and took a few legs off the other two in the practice rooms. It was all pretty easy stuff and great fun, although I hated the theatre lighting – you just couldn't see anything with those bright lights shining in your face. I never knew what I was going to be asked, of course, which was all part of the occasion and I preferred it that way. There was never a case of me having some notes jotted down or anything, just ask me anything and I'll try to give you an answer or a funny story.

Although I wasn't going to be throwing any darts for the foreseeable, I did offer to help out by bringing along a stand and a practice board that could be used in the back rooms wherever we went. I arranged it all with my mate Terry, who has a darts shop in Clacton, but he did have a puzzled look on his face when he brought me the board.

'Smell it Bobby,' he said.

It was a Unicorn board but when I got it out of the box it smelt awful. 'What do you think that is?, he asked.

'It's diesel,' I told him. I reckon when they put colour on the board – screening they call it – they'd mixed the dye with diesel rather than white spirit. The smell was rotten but it was only going to be used for a bit of practice so I took it along anyway and showed Lowey, who is Mr Unicorn. They've been very good to him throughout his career, sponsoring him from the start, so he was always going to stick up for the company.

'You've sprayed that with something,' he proclaimed. 'These are Unicorn boards, so shouldn't smell like that.'

I told him what I thought but he wasn't having any of it.

'Tell me one thing then,' said Eric, laughing towards Lowey. 'How many miles to the gallon do you think we'll get out of it?'

Those shows we did were great fun, due in no small part to the professionalism of Duncan, a hugely talented man who showed me another of his skills one evening. We'd arrived at the venue nice and early and whilst waiting for the others he went through all his sound checks. Throwing a tape to the sound guy, he asked him to pop it on and when the music began Duncan suddenly burst into song. What a singer he was, a wonderful voice. I was genuinely impressed and told him so, adding that I thought it was a good idea if he introduced a bit of singing into the show, maybe to entertain for a few minutes during the break.

'Do you reckon?' he enquired. I told him that I was all for it. A couple of hours later John, Eric and myself were in the back room during the interval and I heard Duncan start singing out on the stage. Up went Lowey's antenna, 'What's that? Who's that singing?' he said.

'It's Duncan,' I told him. 'He's very good, isn't he?'

I'll always remember Lowey's reaction. 'Who gave him permission to sing? He's taking over the show.'

It was a pathetic response really and I told him so. Duncan had got a good voice and he was entertaining the audience during the break. The show was going well and they were all lapping it up.

'I don't like it, I don't like it at all. He's got to go,' continued the three-time Champion of the World.

It was laughable really, 'Got to go, what are you on about, you idiot?' I asked.

'I'm not having it.'

The trouble was, Lowey was actually being serious and I knew that if he got his teeth into an issue he'd not let it go until he'd either got rid of Duncan or stopped him singing. Eric stayed out of it, he'd gone to smoke a rollie and left us arguing. I thought it wise to tip Duncan off and I got my chance the next evening, just before we started. 'Oh, he wants to get rid of me, does he? Just wait until I interview him tonight,' smirked the comic.

So, when it came to the point in the show where Duncan was doing his interviews, he surprised John Lowe in the most marvellous of ways.

'So John,' he began, luring him in. 'I didn't realise you could sing like Johnny Cash?'

'I beg your pardon?'

'I've heard you can sing like Johnny Cash, be great if you could give us a blast. Start the music please ...'

A wall of sound blasted out from the speakers and Lowe suddenly found himself in a potentially embarrassing position.

To be fair to him though, he had a go.

'I fell into a burnin' ring of fire,' he croaked. 'I went down, down, down and the flames went higher.'

The audience were in a mixture of disbelief and hysterics, whilst Eric and I were killing ourselves as we watched from the wings. Duncan had done a right number on him and made him look like a prick.

Lowey came off stage and stormed towards us two, 'That bastard, he's made me look a c**t out there.'

'That's not hard,' I uttered, whilst crying with laughter because he'd been done over properly.

But that wasn't the end of it. The next night, when Duncan was doing his bit with John, he again mentioned that he'd heard what a good singer he was.

Lowey wasn't going to fall for that again. 'No, no I used to do a bit but I retired from singing yesterday,' he announced.

'Yes, I've heard,' tormented Duncan. 'But I've heard that Michael Jackson thinks you're a great dancer.'

'Eh?'

'Michael Jackson thinks you're a great dancer and said he was so impressed with you in that video for "Thriller", because he didn't have to spend anything on clothes or make-up.'

Lowey walked off stage. He knew he couldn't compete with a professional comedian who was taking the piss out of him.

It signalled the end of the tour though because Lowey wouldn't let it rest. 'That's it, he's got to go.'

I made my intentions clear immediately and told them if Duncan went then so would I. You can't be having just darts as your only entertainment because the darts were shit. Duncan brought the comedy, the variety and his interviewing skills, whilst we played the darts and delivered the stories. We were playing to full houses and everyone was leaving with a smile on their face but Lowe's ego killed it for everyone.

I was serious, I wasn't going to do any more shows without Duncan, so the other two brought Bob Anderson in to try to keep the tour alive and they did a few nights before it was all scrapped. It was such a shame because we'd assembled a format that worked and not for the first time, Lowey thought he knew best.

TOOT-TOOT-TOOTSIE BYE-BYE

I MENTIONED a little earlier that I'd had some toes removed. Nobody believes me, or at least they don't until they see me without my socks on, or if they come to my bar in George Hall and see the evidence for themselves.

There's some sort of gene in my body that has caused the toes to pop out of their socket and cross over. It got so bad that I couldn't get my shoes on and I couldn't walk without checking my balance each step. It was so painful on some days that if I'd had a sharp enough knife I'd have chopped them off myself.

There was nothing that the medical profession could do, so it became 'Operation Toot-Toot-Tootsie Bye-Bye'.

The first one was cut off in 1999 and it was actually a great relief when it was all over. I knew the surgeon, a bloke called Phil, and he talked me through the procedure – something called a tulip operation. It's done under local anaesthetic, so I was able to watch him cut it off; it didn't hurt or anything and once the deed was done Phil showed it to me and I asked him if I could keep it. The nurse who had been present went, 'errgh' at the thought of me taking it home. I couldn't understand her reaction. She'd been totally professional and very matter-of-fact whilst it was being cut off, yet looked all squeamish at the thought of me taking it away as a souvenir. Phil presented it to me in a little jar but said that he couldn't give me the proper stuff – formaldehyde, maybe? – as it was poisonous, but if I used vodka instead, that would preserve it beautifully.

So, I took it home and popped it in some vodka and now it has a permanent home behind the bar in George Hall. Whenever anyone comes to the house for a drink I whip it out and ask them if they want a cocktail or a cocktoe? It's also meant that over the years if I've been away from home for any length of time then if Marie is missing me she can always suck my toe!

Removing one tootsie wasn't enough though and eventually the procedure had to be repeated another three times, so I'm missing two toes on each foot. Unfortunately, none of the other surgeons have been as obliging as Phil, and they wouldn't let me take the sawn-off digits away with me, although the last time I went I decided to get circumcised at the same time and they did let me keep that; it's behind the bar in a bucket!

Losing four toes hasn't been as bad as it may sound, although when I go barefoot I do look like an alien. Apart from the missing digits and my broken back, I've also had a number of other fairly major operations and had quite a lengthy list of ailments.

The most serious occurred in 1981 whilst I was in Stockton-on-Tees for the Unipart British Championships. I roomed with Jocky that weekend and will always be grateful that my little mate wasn't too boozed up to notice how poorly I was. Suffering from stomach pain and sweating profusely, I'd visited a doctor a few days before, only to be told I'd 'probably got a bug'.

It felt much worse on the Saturday. I managed to win my match but during the night it got so bad that Jocky called a doctor. Once more I was told it was nothing serious and given some pain relief to get me through until morning. Jocky was still concerned, so fetched Andrea Hanson, girlfriend of Alan Glazier and a former nurse. By this stage I was properly out of it, and Andrea later said that she thought the blood had stopped pumping around my body. She called an ambulance and I was rushed to the Hemington hospital in Cleveland, where they diagnosed a ruptured spleen and severe internal bleeding. My spleen had swollen to 20 times its normal size and had burst. Without putting too fine a point on it, the surgeon said I was an hour away from death if he hadn't operated when he did.

It took a long time to recover from that and I was advised to take a complete rest from darts for six months, ruling me out of a trip to New Zealand to compete in the World Cup of Darts as a member of the England side. Moreover, the medication I was on was so strong that I was banned from consuming any alcohol. For a good couple of years afterwards all I drank was either R White's lemonade or milk.

I drove a Rolls-Royce at the time and one night I'd been doing an exhibition in Liverpool when I was stopped by the police. This copper asked me if I'd been drinking, so I told him I'd had 15 pints. He then proceeded to breathalyse me and was clearly disappointed when nothing showed up. He asked me to do it again and of course it was the same outcome.

'What have you been drinking?' he enquired.

'Lemonade.'

'You didn't tell me that,' he said.

'You didn't ask!'

I've since had my hips and knees done as more and more bits of my body have packed up. Most of the ailments have been caused through sheer hard work, I reckon. Quite simply I wore my body out. I wasn't very clever in the early part of my life, using my physical strength to earn money and it makes me walk like a monkey sometimes.

One night Marie and I went to see the film *Planet of the Apes*. It's a two and a half hour movie and when it finished I tried to get up but couldn't stand up straight … I was walking like one of the monkeys. My missus said, 'Behave, what are you doing, taking the mickey out of the film?'

I'd got to the foyer by that time and some dickhead threw a net over me and dragged me off to Colchester Zoo for the night.

THOSE PEARLY WHITES

ALTHOUGH MIKE Gregory didn't get a chance to feature in the televised League of Legends tournament, he does feature in one of my funniest memories of playing on the European circuit.

One year I was playing pairs in Germany with John Boy Walton and had a good run – we may have been beaten in the final, something like that. We'd had a good day, anyway, and hailed a taxi to take us somewhere to get some food and a celebratory drink or two. We piled into the cab and so did one or two others and then, with the car rammed full of people, I saw Mike waiting on his own. I shouted for him to come and join us and somehow we got him in, sprawled across the laps of everybody in the back seat and then away we went.

At the restaurant I noticed that Mike had gaps in his teeth and asked him about them. He said that he'd gone to play in the Belgian Open and when he got into a lift, a chap took one look at Mike and then smacked him, knocking a tooth out in what turned out to be a case of mistaken identity.

Then he went to another tournament where he'd over-celebrated and had another tooth knocked out by a disgruntled opponent.

'Blimey Mike,' I said. 'Are you going to play in the Worlds this year, mate?'

'No,' was his blunt response.

'What about other ranking tournaments, you're still playing, right?'

Again, he said that he wasn't, so I asked him why.

'Because I've not got enough teeth to go round,' he said, as we both burst into laughter.

Another story concerning some pearly whites involves a former Embassy World Champion, Scotland's second to win the title after Jocky. Les Wallace won the 1997 event at the Lakeside, defeating Marshall James of Wales. A lovely bloke, Les liked to wear his kilt and be accompanied to the stage by bagpipes and was someone who enjoyed a Friday night out as much as anyone I've ever met.

'I'm on the case,' he used to say. 'I'm on the case Bobby,' which almost certainly meant he was going out on the lash.

However, one particular Friday night he got into a row with someone and had a bit of a ruck, which resulted in his front two teeth getting knocked out. The dentist sorted him out with a couple of temporary ones but they didn't last long as he ended up having another disagreement and they were knocked out as well. When it happened for a third time – some folks never learn, do they? – he decided that he ought to have something more permanent put in and paid a dentist top dollar prices to sort him out.

A week or two later he was at a tournament somewhere and one of his mates said he was just nipping over the road to get some Kentucky Fried Chicken (KFC to you youngsters).

'Get me some as well,' said Les, who went by the nickname of 'McDanger'.

Fifteen minutes later he was tucking into his meal and looked up. Everyone started laughing. 'Where's your teeth, Les?' they asked. He'd only gone and swallowed his expensive replacements. I'm told that nature eventually took its course and he got them back a little later. Ouch. I assume the dentist had thought he'd never see Les again.

Speaking of our Scottish friends, another Jocky story springs to mind. One year when we were heading off to play in America I happened to lift Jocky's suitcase up at the airport and discovered it was ridiculously light. When I asked him about it he said that he'd only got a pair of socks in it. The trip was going to be about four weeks in length, so I questioned him about what he was going to wear for all of that time. 'Don't worry Bobby,' he said. 'I'll buy what I need out of my winnings!'

You have to admire his confidence, if not his suitcase. It was horrible, well and truly battered, with the blue paint peeling off.

'Why are you taking this old thing with you anyway?' I wanted to know.

'Because it looks better when you check in at a hotel if you've got a suitcase with you.' You couldn't argue with his logic.

I think that was the year that we played a lot of pairs together. It would get awkward at times because we'd be playing and winning throughout the day and by the time we got through to the final and got on the stage he'd be well and truly tanked up. It was hard enough to understand him at the best of times but by the time you'd got that far, it would be like he was conversing in another language.

He could also be very easily confused. One event that springs to mind was when we got through to the pairs final at the Los Angeles Open. I threw first and started off with 100, they got 60, then Jocky got 100, they got 85, this went on for a couple more throws and then my fiery partner yelled, 'Cheating bastard!' and ran over and started to thump the chalker, who was standing on the left-hand side of the board. Bloody hell. I leapt in to drag him off this poor chap and Big Cliff Lazarenko jumped on the stage as well to hold Jocky back with me.

'What's the matter with you?' I growled at him.

'He's cheating Bobby, he's fucking cheating,' screamed the wild-eyed Scot.

A quick glance at the scores was all I needed. 'No, he's not. Jocky, we're on the right-hand side, this is their score you dickhead!'

That wasn't the only time I saw him do that, either. Mind you, one day he was the one who got clobbered. We were doing an exhibition somewhere in Scotland, just me and him and it was packed. In the interval a queue formed for autographs. Now Jocky was no oil painting himself but this old lady started coming on to him and she was hideous, really ugly, bless her. She looked like a witch, with warts all over her face.

'Give us a wee kiss,' she whispered in my mate's ear.

He backed away and tried to ignore her but she was persistent, she wanted a kiss from her favourite player. Still

Jocky was having none of it before eventually snapping, 'Eh missus, is that your husband?'

After she'd confirmed it was, Jocky said, 'In that case I'd rather kiss him.'

Upon hearing that, this woman suddenly swung her handbag and smacked him hard around the head. She'd caught him completely off guard and his head was ringing for ages afterwards.

'She only wanted a wee kiss,' I laughed at him.

RICHIE RICH

WHILST MY chances of winning the BDO World Championship were well behind me, the family dream of lifting the famous old trophy was revived in 2013 when my youngest son Richard qualified for Lakeside. Both Robert and Richard had grown up with a dart in their hand and by the age of two both knew their way around a dartboard as well as anyone. As they grew older they spent thousands of hours practising alongside me and working out their finishes; we'd have some right old battles between us.

Playing with my two I could see how darts was helping them with their maths and it gave me some food for thought as to how it could help others.

Around the same time I was invited to go along to their school and give a chat to the pupils about my career. I didn't think they would be that interested in hearing me talk about winning the *News of the World* Championship or how many pints of Guinness Eric would sup in one session, so I looked at how a simple dartboard might be able to help them. They were only young kids but I figured out that I could show them around the board and it might help one or two with their basic maths. So, I took along a freestanding board and we split them into small groups and helped them understand the different segments on the board. Removing the 25 and bullseye from the equation, the rest of the board is all about multiples of six.

A single, double and treble 1 add up to six; a single, double and treble 2 add up to 12; the 3s equal 18 and so on. Basic stuff to grasp and I'm pleased to say that many of them had that lightbulb moment when suddenly they could work out some simple maths, just by looking at the board. We gave them a number of relatively easy sums to do and enjoyed watching them solve the puzzles.

I hoped it had been of some use, so was delighted when a couple of weeks later I was invited to go back. We went into the assembly room and there was a video playing of one of my televised matches. I didn't even recognise what tournament it was, so had to ask a teacher if I won this one.

'Yes,' he laughed.

The children gave me a big cheer then the headmaster announced that since my previous visit he'd given them all a short maths test on the stuff they'd learned with me and they'd all done well. The head was beaming and came across and thanked me and I actually felt quite chuffed that I'd been able to help.

Following on from that, we did a video for the Teachers Channel, so it got some nationwide exposure and was beneficial to youngsters all over the land. Locally, a few surrounding schools in areas like Halstead and Manningtree invited me in to talk to their pupils and again we got great feedback. It's a shame really that I didn't have enough time to do more but it was a very rewarding experience to know that a combination of some simple logic and a standard dartboard had been of help.

I'm not sure why it took so long, but around 30 years after I'd started doing it, off my own bat, I heard that the PDC were getting players into schools to do something similar. Hopefully today's youngsters will enjoy it as much as my groups did.

Robert could have been a very decent player but chose not to go in that direction, although he enjoyed playing youth darts for Essex for a while. A bit like his old man, he has been able to turn his hand to anything and became a self-employed carpenter, earning his money by going into new-builds and doing the doors, roofs and skirting boards before the other trades come in and get to work. He loves the outdoor life and grows all his own vegetables and keeps chickens and tortoises and all sorts of pets. He's also a very good artist.

His younger brother did give darts a real go and at the age of 13 or 14 qualified for the Youth Winmau World Masters, a prestigious competition for young players. Richard was so excited but it was a tough time for him; there was so much going on as he'd just been diagnosed with type one diabetes and it took time for his body to adjust to the changes that having the insulin causes.

By the age of 16 he was playing county darts for Essex and at England Youth level but then he took some time away, concentrating on building up a business, before regaining an appetite for darts. Winning some big local open events like the Colchester Open and the Southend Open gave him that bit of belief and a passport into the 2012 World Masters. There, he made it through to the last 32 before losing out on television to Thomas Junghans of Switzerland.

Things were going well for Richard and he qualified for Lakeside the following year, with Mike Walters popping in lots of family references when writing a preview piece about it in the *Daily Mirror*:

> *'Prince of Dartness' Richie George follows his father Bobby on to the Lakeside stage crowing: 'Bling it on.'*
>
> *George, 23, becomes the first son to follow his father into the main draw at a world darts championship when he faces Dave Prins at the British Darts Organisation's party in Frimley Green.*
>
> *George, following in the footsteps of the self-styled King of Darts – Bobby George took to the stage in crown, cloak, candelabra and dripping with jewellery – is history the PDC can't match.*
>
> *The bling is dead, long live the bling.*
>
> *George II said: 'It is a privilege to go to the Lakeside as a player for the first time because I kind of grew up there and it's nice to be following in dad's footsteps. I'm trying to not let it affect me because Lakeside is such a big tournament.*
>
> *'I do have dad's personality – I like a laugh and enjoy myself playing darts, but I'm not into his bling. What I have to do is make a name for myself. It would be great to win it, not just for me but for dad as he never won Lakeside.'*

There was bound to be lots of interest in how Richard got on after my achievements in the event but he shrugged them to one side and survived two match darts on his debut before eventually getting the better of Dave Prins by three sets to two.

Then he defeated two Dutch players, Jimmy Hendrix 4-2 and Jan Dekker 5-4, having trailed 1-3, to advance to the last four. His winning streak ended at the semi-final stage, sadly, when he lost to Scott Waites, but he'd done himself no harm at all and we were all so proud of his performances.

Over the next couple of years Marie and I went and watched him compete in a number of top-level events, including the World Trophy, the World Masters, a 2014 return to Lakeside and a couple of Grand Slam of Darts events at Wolverhampton, where he came within a whisker of defeating former PDC World Champion Adrian Lewis.

Whilst we call him Richard within the family his darting nickname ended up being 'Richie Rich', a good name to have on the back of your shirt. I joke that I called him that because he used to spend all of my money but Marie says it's because as a young lad in the school holidays he would always go and work on the farm over the road. He would cut lettuces for them, morning, noon and night and ended up saving two or three grand.

I was often asked what it was like watching him play and if I was nervous for him. Like any dad, I was just immensely proud, like I am of all the family. There were occasions when I felt for him, perhaps more than I should have. During the World Masters I felt he was cheated out of the competition, when the referee called game shot on a dart from Ryan Searle that wasn't in the double. You know when you throw – and certainly when you go up to the board to retrieve your darts – whether it's in the winning double or not. Richard may not have won that day but either the referee or his opponent should have taken a step back and realised that it wasn't in the double. That's no way to be knocked out of such a prestigious event.

Richard won some decent events including the Dutch Pairs and was offered a tour card by the PDC, but turned it down as other things in his life were starting to gain more importance. It wasn't really a surprise then, when he came home one day, chucked his darts on the bar and said, 'That's it, I'm not playing anymore.' He felt he'd done all he wanted to do and he now works as a plumbing and heating engineer.

At every exhibition I go to, even after all this time, I'm still asked how 'Richie Rich' is and if he's going to return to big-time darts. I suspect that it's unlikely but we are both very proud that we are still the only father and son to have both played in the Lakeside World Championships.

WALK-ON BY

SOME OF the darts walk-ons have become iconic over the years, with the biggest characters making grand entrances into the country's largest arenas.

It all had to start somewhere though and the first time that a player walked on to any music was when I did it for the BDO World Championships at the Lakeside in 1994. Eric Bristow had tried once or twice to marry his 'Crafty Cockney' persona to the National Anthem. Can you imagine, walking out to that and hoping it would inspire a darts audience? I told him to forget it as it sounded awful and made everything feel a bit flat when you're trying to do the opposite and create an atmosphere.

I'd been giving some serious thought to how I could improve my walk-ons and when I got through to the semi-finals I really wanted to give it some oomph and inject some atmosphere and fun into the crowd, getting them singing along to something catchy whilst I walked on. I mentioned my thoughts to a cameraman called Bob Wilson and the BBC and the BDO agreed that it was a good idea.

Martin Fitzmaurice, the MC, whispered to me, 'Stand by for the music, Glitter' (that's what he always called me) as I prepared for my entrance. So, there I was, waiting to be introduced ahead of a world semi-final and wondering just what sort of racket would accompany me to the stage. Then I heard the first few strains begin to boom out …

'Come on, come on, come on, come on …'

Fair play, Gary Glitter giving it plenty with 'Do you wanna be in my gang, my gang, my gang?' got them off their seats and the place was absolutely rocking as I made my way to the stage. You need to remember that Glitter had been an enormous star in the 1970s and this was one of his biggest hits and had peaked at number one all over Europe. There wasn't a soul inside Lakeside who didn't know the words and they loved belting it out on live television.

Also, it's worth noting that this was a number of years before that particular artist was convicted of sexual abuse and his music became untouchable. No one wanted to be associated with it or him after that.

Everyone began to talk about my walk-on though and it wasn't long before the other players started to up their game and have their own introductory music. For reasons of good taste and decency it became necessary to change my music very early on, and I decided to go with the Queen hit, 'We Are the Champions'. It's a great crowd-pleaser, guaranteed to get them all swaying and singing and it's long enough for me to make my way from the practice rooms to the stage with plenty of unscheduled stop-offs to pose for photos and join in with the singalongs.

My entrances have become so notorious that nowadays it's all that people care about. They're not bothered about seeing me hit the board anymore, they just want to witness the greatest walk-on in darts for themselves. Crackers, isn't it? I get bookings just to walk to the stage, whilst others only get paid for what they do once they're on it.

The proper advent of 'Bobby the Showman' all developed from those early walk-ons and my image was soon transformed to complement my new music.

To the modern generation, top-flight darts revolves around certain gimmicks and I've been responsible for many of them: the glittery shirts, walk-on music, flamboyant entrances and the like. The sequinned shirts didn't come cheap, mind you – they were all handmade and cost the best part of £100 each – a lot of money to fork out just to look good on the telly back in the 1980s.

At exhibitions, if I did a particularly flashy outshot or something I would occasionally lift my shirt up and 'flex my pecs' – something I've been able to do since getting into reasonable shape through all the hard graft I used to do. It was a little bit of harmless fun and made people laugh. Over time, the sight of me lifting my shirt up might have become less palatable but a lady called Louise Florence – the cousin of Little Richard Ashdown – suggested an alternative idea. Why didn't I have a 'false pocket' put into my shirt fronts? Rather than lifting the whole shirt up I could just pull down the pocket and waggle the nipple about instead.

Sharon Mitchell, wife of former BDO World Champion Scott and a close family friend, is a dab hand at sewing and embroidery and set to work on developing her prototype –

'Bobby's Boob', as it became known. The pocket would always have some catchy little slogan on it: 'Helloooo' was always a favourite, or 'Could You, Should You, Would You?'

There were one or two people who didn't get the joke. Mervyn King was one of the players that didn't go a lot on it but it brought a few laughs wherever I went and that's what it's all about, isn't it? In the end, England even had one made up for me with 'God Save the Queen' on the pocket!

Nowadays, it just wouldn't be a Bobby George walk-on without the flowing cape, the candelabra and the gold rings. That's when I'm being the King of Bling or the Showman or Mr Glitter or whatever; that's the working me, the stage persona, my public calling card. Away from the darts venues though, folks tend to forget that I'm just plain old Robert George. You'd be surprised how many times I'm stopped when I go to the shops with Marie or am out somewhere minding my own business, and people ask where the cloak and candles are!

Can you imagine it?

Even at the darts, when I'm making my way through the crowd, with music blaring out of the speakers and me in my cloak and carrying my candelabra I think, 'You wally, what must you look like?'

I feel like Del Boy running down Peckham High Street wearing his Batman gear.

LIGHTS, CAMERA, ACTION

SINCE RETIRING from competitive darts, I've been very fortunate to have had plenty of offers to get involved with all sorts of television projects. Towards the end of my first book, I mentioned some of the stuff I'd started to do, including a series of the show *Celebrity Fit Club*, where I managed to lose almost three stones. My old darting mate Andy Fordham also did that show and lost a similar amount of weight, so the TV execs knew we were good as gold. Give us a project and we'd crack on and do it.

They invited the pair of us to be team captains on a programme called *Showbiz Darts*. The idea was that we'd each try to teach four well-known personalities how to play darts and then they would compete against each other. My four celebrities were presenter Holly Willoughby, former cricketer Phil Tufnell, Michael Le Vell, who is best known as Kevin Webster in *Coronation Street*, and James Hewitt, the army officer who at one time was rumoured to be romantically linked with Diana, Princess of Wales.

Andy took his quartet back to the pub he ran in Woolwich but I invited my four over to George Hall, to practise and stay with us for the duration of the filming.

On the first day Holly came to practice in a lovely pair of flat sandals. The trouble was they had no support to them, so were totally inappropriate for walking to and from the dartboard.

It made me chuckle and I told her, 'You can't wear those, doll.' But she cracked on and gave it her best shot, as did all the others. I'd met Tuffers a few times at dinners and sports events and we'd always enjoyed a few laughs together. James Hewitt was a lovely bloke, a real gentleman. Very polite, very well-mannered, it was easy to see why any young lady would be attracted to him.

Michael was the most pleasant surprise – because he was good, really good. He put himself out for the duration of the programme and really applied himself to his darts. I gave him a few tips and helped him with his finishing and it was no surprise to me when he got through and made it all the way to the final, beating the best of Andy's team, comedian Johnny Vegas. I think everyone enjoyed themselves and it made for some decent light-hearted television, screened over a few weeks.

Another TV show I was involved in around that time was a celebrity version of the popular daytime programme, *Cash in the Attic*. Most of you will have seen it, I'm sure. When members of the public take part it's to try to raise a few quid for their own benefit. Antiques experts have a snoop around your house, recommend anything that might make a few quid at auction and away they go, hoping that the old vase your granny gave you 30 years ago might be worth a fortune.

They asked if I might be interested in taking part in a celebrity special, with any money raised donated to charity. Like most folks, my wife Marie and I are always threatening to have a good clear-out of stuff that we've packed away in boxes, in the garage or the attic, and never got round to it. I thought it an ideal opportunity for a sort-out and to do something for a good cause.

My old mate Roly Bright, who is sadly no longer with us, used to do a lot of work helping youngsters with learning disabilities. For many years Roly would come on the road with me, as my driver and as the MC for some of my exhibitions. As well as being the chairman of Suffolk darts, he was a scoutmaster and had a heart of gold. He helped out, when he could, at the MENCAP centre at Woodbridge and I thought it appropriate that anything we raised could go and help them. They relied heavily on donations and with a few extra quid they could take the kids on a few trips and feed them whilst they were out.

Angela Rippon presented the show and came round with valuations expert John Cameron and their film crew to decide on which items they thought might go well at auction. There were all sorts of bits and bobs from around the house and I also decided to have a bit of a clear-out of some of the darts memorabilia I'd hung on to for years.

I had made my England debut in the Home Internationals in Edinburgh back in 1979 and was very proud of the shirt I'd worn that day, plus my England blazer and trousers. For sentiment, I suppose, I'd hung on to them for all these years but this seemed like a good opportunity to let them go.

John had a look around in a few boxes and found some fun items. There was a pair of sparkly glasses that had been made by someone and given to me years ago. Attached to the rims, above each eye, were the words Bob and George. I hit a 180 in the World Championship and popped them on to look down the camera for a bit of fun; the crowd loved it.

Also in the box was a copy of the record I did back in 1981. I'm sure all 'music' lovers will remember '180' and the equally catchy B-side, 'Bobby's Theme'.

To be fair to John, he was certainly clued up and asked me about a set of silver-barrelled darts he'd spotted. They'd been made in 1937 and were given to me years ago by someone who'd bought them from an antiques shop. Hollowed out, they were certainly unusual but I had no need to hang on to them.

The early years of the World Championships – the Embassy-sponsored era – was undoubtedly a golden period for the sport and I'd kept a few programmes, photographs and signed pictures from those days and they all went into making up another lot for auction.

One of the true stars in the early days of televised darts was Leighton Rees.

The loveable Welsh international had won the first World Championship back in 1978 and we'd always enjoyed each other's company. Somewhere over a beer or two he'd given me one of his shirts and had signed his picture on the front cover of a *Darts World* magazine. Taken from us far too early, I thought that there'd be quite a lot of interest from his fans for these items.

I also threw in another of my shirts, one that had several major tournament patches sewn on, something you were given when you qualified for the World Masters or the World Championship. Along with some ornamental figures, old clocks and some gold-coloured napkin rings I'd been presented with at some tournament somewhere, there was a decent number of items to take to auction.

We were told that it might take a few months to properly advertise the items and get them to auction but the programme was running to a tight deadline and it was all rushed through in just a couple of weeks, which didn't really help. John had put an estimate of around £400 on all the different lots but I thought they should go for a bit more than that. Certainly, in this day and age with the interest in sports memorabilia and everyone having access to the internet and being able to bid from all around the world, I think we'd have got a lot more.

In the end we managed to raise £522, so I put a brave face on it – although I still thought that was a bit cheap for some of the stuff. Still, the centre were more than made up when we took the money round to them and it went towards giving the kids a bit of a treat. Lovely jubbly.

One of the lasting things from doing that programme has been that John Cameron and I have remained in touch and he's even brought his son for a day's fishing at George Hall.

Any money I made from television appearances around that time went to that MENCAP centre. One such show was titled *Don't Call Me Stupid*, where 16 celebrities were pitted against one another, and each had to learn a favourite passion of the other. I was paired with journalist and presenter Vanessa Feltz.

Rather than selecting darts, the obvious choice, I challenged Vanessa to learn all about my other great passion, fishing. She had three months to learn all sorts of information, the different species, places where they could be caught, that sort of thing. She came over to the house and we got on like a house on fire and she made me laugh when she swore at a cameraman. She taught me some words I've never heard before. Then it was time to discover my subject for *Don't Call Me Stupid.*

I was gobsmacked as Vanessa revealed that her passion was the works of Geoffrey Chaucer and my challenge was to learn as much as I could about the life and times of the great British poet and author. My immediate thought was, 'How can that be a passion?'

I've never been top of the class when it comes to things like that, but I thought, 'Fuck it. If I'm doing this then I'm going to do it properly and have a good crack at it.'

First of all I was given a package, which contained a kiddies-type book all about *The Canterbury Tales*, then I really started to get into it.

I got hold of a CD and listened to some of his stuff then decided to make a trip down to Kent to have a look around the town and learn some more bits and pieces. I didn't think I'd ever be studying Chaucer at my time of life but the more I got into it, the more I thought he was a bit like me! He wasn't averse to being a bit rude and his language, like mine, could be a little fruity. In those days it wasn't the done thing to talk about your bollocks or your arsehole but he did and seemed to enjoy doing it as well.

Thanks to Chaucer, many hours of motorway driving seemed to fly by on the way to darts exhibitions as I read out some of his stuff to Roly Bright, my driver. Chaucer wrote passages in his own special lingo, sort of a Cockney rhyming slang, and when I read it out loud, with a bit of Bobby George spin on it, Roly would absolutely piss himself with laughter. He'd be almost crying and would punch the dashboard as he drove along. It was so funny seeing him like that and he'd say that Chaucer was the Bobby George of his time – or was I the modern-day Chaucer? What a fucking cheek!

We'd speculate about what questions I might be asked on the programme and if they'd mention some of his more sensitive works.

'Who cares,' I'd say. 'The Romans didn't bother, they'd have a dump next to each other, then pass along a sponge on a stick to wipe your arse.'

It was nothing to do with Chaucer, of course, but it would set Roly off laughing again and keep our spirits up as we travelled around the country.

When the programme was aired we found out for the first time who had won. Poor old Vanessa, I think she'd found fishing a little bit tougher than she'd imagined and to her total surprise, I was declared the winner.

Something must have struck a chord with me about good old Geoffrey Chaucer. A shrewd bloke but very clever, was he the Bobby George of his day?

WALK THIS WAY

ONE YEAR I was approached to go on the BBC charity fundraising show, *Let's Dance for Sport Relief*, with fellow darts professional Tony O'Shea and snooker stars Willie Thorne and Dennis Taylor. To call us a dance act would be stretching it a bit, but the judging panel was made up of comedians Jason Manford and Frank Skinner, plus Girls Aloud singer Kimberley Walsh, with Claudia Winkleman as the presenter.

Willie and Dennis were dressed up as the flamboyant Steve Tyler and Joe Perry from the rock band Aerosmith, whilst Tony and me were supposed to be rappers, with the gold chains and smart jackets on. Mine had Dazzler on the back and he had his Silverback nickname on the back of his.

It was all good fun; they got the four of us together the day before the event and we had two or three sessions to rehearse what we were going to do – our take on the Run DMC hit song, 'Walk This Way'.

We were all staying together and once we'd got the dance sorted, I said, 'Right lads, what are we doing this evening?' thinking we'd have a couple of pints somewhere or something like that. Dennis and Willie revealed that they were going to the Ritz for a meal. It wasn't particularly what I'd got in mind but I wouldn't want to be accused of not being sociable, so said I'd tag along.

I wasn't prepared for the reply.

'I'm sorry, you can't,' said Willie. 'We'd lose our membership if we took you.'

The posh gits. I couldn't believe it but I had the last laugh the next morning at breakfast when they revealed they'd been charged £300 for some fish and chips and wine. Served 'em right!

I was still laughing when we went and recorded our piece. It couldn't have gone much better, even though at the end Dennis and me both lost our way and ended up tripping over each other and we all fell in a heap. It was unscripted but worked so much better than the original ending, so they left it in.

Much as we'd had a laugh, I don't think any of us were either surprised or too disappointed when the panel didn't put us through to the next round. Still, you can't legislate for people not having any taste! I don't think Dennis and I could have collapsed as spectacularly as we had the first time, in any case. We'd all enjoyed it immensely; it was great fun and all for a worthy cause.

Some television jobs are less demanding than others. An invitation to take a small role in Sean Lock's sitcom, *15 Storeys High* wasn't exactly taxing. Sean's character had been put into some stocks, as a form of punishment. All I had to do was walk up and throw some rotten tomatoes at him. I've done some harder graft in my time!

When you do stuff like that you never really know what sort of reaction, if any, it will get from the general public. One bit of work I did went down much better than expected.

Richard Hammond hosted a programme called *Brainiac – Science Abuse*, based, you won't be surprised to hear, on doing various scientific experiments. They wanted me to come on the show and throw darts, with the outcome of each throw deciding the fate of an old caravan. They had me dressed up looking like James Bond in sunglasses and whenever I hit a combination and finished it with a double top, a caravan would be blown up.

It was staged at the drag racing track at Santa Pod in Northamptonshire and my old mate Tony Green, the former darts MC and commentator, came along with me. It was great fun and certainly captured the attention of the viewers.

For weeks afterwards I would get mail asking me about it. Very often it was just addressed to Bobby George, The Man Who Blew Caravans Up, Essex. It made a change to get correspondence from people wanting to talk about that programme rather than the usual requests for any old spare darts flights.

I also featured on a reality programme called *Don't Tell the Bride*, which went out on Channel 4 and was hugely popular. Prospective grooms were given a budget and left to arrange the entire wedding in secret. His bride knew she was getting married but that was about all.

My involvement started without my knowing. Whilst I was in hospital having my knee done, Marie took a phone call at home from a young man called Liam. He told her that he was an avid darts fans and he wanted to have a darts-themed wedding with me conducting the ceremony. Marie obviously told him that I was in hospital at the time, so once I was back home the television company arranged for him to come and see me at home, with them there filming it.

Liam came in and said, 'Bobby, will you marry me?'

It's not every day you get an offer like that, is it? I said, 'Give us a kiss and I'll tell ya!'

None of it made much sense to me at the time. I wondered if I'd fully recovered from my anaesthetic! Liam went on to say that he wanted to marry his bride, Chelsey, at the Lakeside Country Club, home for many years of the BDO World Championships. The idea was that the place would be decked out as if it was holding a darts tournament and they would get married on the stage.

I laughed and wished him all the best with it but he was insistent that he wanted me to marry them.

'I'm not a priest or anything,' I told him. 'You have to be ordained or something to do that.' He was clearly under the impression that I had the authority to join them in holy matrimony and then the TV producers intervened and before I knew it they were issuing me with a certificate from the Minister for the Universal Church of Life granting me the power to conduct weddings.

So, it was all set and a couple of weeks later I was on my way to the Lakeside to conduct my first marriage ceremony, accompanied by my MC at the time, Paul Starr.

I was there in good time but they wanted me to play a cruel prank on Liam and ring him to say I was held up in traffic. 'I'm sorry mate, I don't think I can make it,' I told him. 'I didn't expect the traffic to be this bad, I'm still about four hours away.'

Poor lad, he was obviously close to tears and kept saying, 'What can I do, what can I do?'

Once they'd recorded their little bit of drama I was able to put Liam's mind at rest and assure him I was there already, sat out in the car park.

Inside the venue, they'd set it up magnificently, as if it was ready to host the World Championships. Darting posters, banners and photos were everywhere and the stage was set up, complete with the oche, mat and a single board. All exactly as Liam would have wanted. I was whisked off to a backstage dressing room to get ready and popped on a sequinned cape for the ceremony.

Looking the business, complete with my candelabra, I had to do my duty and make sure I didn't let the happy couple down. Not wanting to get my lines wrong, I'd put my glasses on and read them over and over but was still feeling very nervous as we waited to get going. The place was filling up with family and friends and I told a few stories to keep them entertained. Then we got the green light that Chelsey was ready to make her entrance and the music began to play.

I'd worked with a couple of the telly boys before and nodded to a couple of the camera crew. Liam and Chelsey were ushered towards me on stage and I asked the best man if he'd got the rings.

'They're behind you,' he said, like a kid at a pantomime. I looked towards the board and in the bullseye two wedding rings were held in place by a single dart without the flight on.

One of the rings was visibly much larger than the other. I said something that I probably shouldn't have but they cut it out from the TV edit, although I wished they'd kept it in.

'Have you got a small ring or a large ring?' I asked Chelsey. One of the cameramen was already pissing himself by this stage and most of the others joined in. To be fair, Chelsey kept her composure and said hers was the small one.

What she made of it all was unclear but we got through the ceremony and I got through the 'legal' bit, eventually pronouncing them man and wife. It was all pretty surreal but I think everyone had a good time and we were all ready for a little drink together afterwards. Since then, whenever I've worked a darts show with Paul Starr I'm reminded of that day as he always introduces me as 'the Reverend!'

Whilst getting me to perform as a member of the clergy might be a bit of a stretch, one or two people had suggested over the years that my east London tones might be more than suitable for a cameo appearance as a villain in *EastEnders*. Sadly, that's still not happened but I have appeared in an episode of *Doctors*, another BBC soap opera. It wasn't the most demanding of roles as I had to play myself, just happening to walk into a pub when the *Doctors* team were having a game of darts. I had quite a few lines, commenting on their shots and talking to a few of the regulars.

The difficult bit was that they were all under the impression that I could just hit anything at will and they used me to do some outshots whenever the players got anywhere near to a double. As the tension grew in the episode, one team required 307 to win. They showed the thrower in action, whilst I was the one landing the 140 – right on cue, as asked.

That left 167 for the next throw of course, and the director was just expecting me to pop that finish out at the first time of asking. I told him that it wasn't always that easy but went to the trouble of making sure that the oche was the required distance as I took aim.

Marie was with me and it had already been a long day by this point. I think she feared that it might take some time for me to complete this finish to order. I'd warned them to keep filming if I hit the treble 20 with my first dart, which I did. Then I hit the treble 19, before taking aim and landing the third dart right in the centre of the bullseye. The tension in the middle of the room had been building and they were all willing me on and the cheers that erupted when I hit the bull were so loud and genuine that they kept them in for the final edit.

Using three fat, chunky darts, that were nothing like my own, it was one of the most satisfying things I've ever done to complete a 167 finish at the first time of asking.

Whilst most dart players are very particular about their own individual darts, we can all make a pretty good show of playing with someone else's if need be. That said, I've rarely seen anything that matches what former BDO World Champ Scott Mitchell did one day at my house. At the side of my practice board he noticed a selection of darts that I'd been gifted over the years and asked if he could use them. The first ones he picked up were an old set of Phil Taylor's. Without any practice or anything, he went 60, 60, 60.

Then he tried a set of Colin Lloyd's and did exactly the same. When he fired in his third consecutive 180, this time with an old set of John Part's, we both looked at each other and wondered what was going on.

Three consecutive 180s with three different sets of darts: neither of us would have believed it had we not seen it with our own eyes. The sequence had to end, of course. Scott popped some flights in his own darts and promptly hit … 45!

INDIA AND BEYOND

MAINLY DUE to my darts I've been very fortunate to travel to some wonderful destinations around the world but there were still a lot of places I'd not been to and fancied visiting. Fortunately, over the last few years, I've been able to tick some of them off.

There was a film released in 2011 called *The Best Exotic Marigold Hotel,* a light-hearted comedy which centred around some British retirees moving to India to see out their twilight years in a warm climate with a more affordable standard of living. Fanciful perhaps but it makes for an interesting debate as to whether such a move could realistically be achieved.

So, inspired by the success of the film, the concept of *The Real Marigold Hotel* was set. I was initially contacted by the talent producer Ros Edwards, who was looking for a 'man of the people' to join the show. She'd been tipped off by her sister Gina, who'd told her to look no further than Bobby George!

Given that build-up I became one of the celebrities who were invited to go to India for a few weeks to see how we'd all get on experiencing the culture and way of life in that country. I'd never been to India before and didn't know who my travel companions would be until we all met up at Heathrow, ahead of the long flight to Jaipur. My fellow travellers were Dr Who actor Sylvester McCoy, Harry Potter star Miriam Margolyes, dancer Wayne Sleep, game show host Roy Walker, chef Rosemary Shrager, singer Patti Boulaye and newsreader Jan Leeming.

Marie and I have always said it would be nice to settle down and spend our retirement in the sun and I was keen to experience how senior citizens would cope living in other countries. Jaipur is the capital city of the state of Rajasthan in northern India and is home to around three and a half million people. It's fairly cheap for westerners to reside there and the hot and dry climate makes it a particularly attractive place to settle down.

Driving from the airport into the city gave us an early indication of how chaotically the locals live their lives. There seems to be no organised structure on the roads, with no one giving way. It's very much every man (or woman) for themselves.

Jaipur is known as the pink city, due to the reddish brick colouring on most of the buildings. The eight of us were all accommodated together in a traditional 160-year-old town house or mansion, called a haveli, which had belonged to the same family for all that time. The idea of the show was that we would try to embrace the way that the Indians lived, to see if we could set down roots there. It was difficult to even imagine it because we were living in very nice accommodation, with chefs, cleaners, drivers and general helpers, whilst we only had to look outside to see less-fortunate people sitting and sleeping on the floor because they didn't have anywhere else to call home.

It really opened my eyes to how some people live, with huge extremes between the haves and have-nots. Some were dripping in wealth and living like kings in their magnificent palaces, whilst others had absolutely nothing, yet they smiled, got on with it and somehow managed to survive.

With cameras following our every move, we adapted very quickly to our new surroundings. Culturally, it was difficult to take in and our regular walks into the heart of the city were a leap of faith. Apart from trying to negotiate your way through a never-ending tide of cars, bikes and motorcycles, you had to be alert to avoid being struck by one of the thousands of tuk-tuks, rickshaws which were used to pedal tourists and travellers around the city. We had many rides in them during our stay and found them to be the most effective way of getting around. Whilst being a tuk-tuk driver would represent regular employment and a liveable wage, it certainly wasn't easy work and was a job where you practically took your life in your hands every single day.

Jaipur's streets weren't solely used by vehicles and pedestrians. Cows, a sacred animal in India, have the freedom to walk anywhere they wish, and these large, placid criminals could soon carve their way through the congested alleyways bumping folks out of the way as they went.

The producers were obviously keen for us to try new things and dive headlong into the local culture and one morning I was up nice and early and went with Jan and Wayne to a local park to experience a different start to the day. It was called laughing yoga and it did what it said on the tin. There were perhaps 20 or 30 of us there and for reasons best known to themselves, everyone would keep bursting into laughter. Jan and Wayne embraced it fully but I couldn't understand for the life of me what they were all laughing at. Stood there laughing at each other? Really? I like a laugh as much as the next person but do it when I find something funny. Not because the clock says it's time to start laughing. Back home, they'd think I was a nutcase and lock me up if I went over to my local park and did that one morning. It's supposed to have health and well-being benefits but it wasn't for me.

We were all keen to make a visit to one of India's most beautiful pieces of architecture, the world-famous Taj Mahal, situated about 150 miles away from us in Agra. Miriam, Rosemary, Wayne, Sylvester and I decided to make the four-hour journey by train whilst the others opted to go by road. Tickets for the five of us cost just £60 in total and it included a bed for each of us. Although the train was badly overcrowded it didn't bother me in the slightest because I slept all the way!

Agra was much hotter than Jaipur, absolutely stifling in fact but it was well worth it. The Taj Mahal is one of the most special places I've ever been to and I wouldn't have missed it for all the world, although I didn't like the history behind it.

Given my background in the building trade the producers of the programme wanted to get my take on some of the properties in Jaipur that were currently available to rent. On some of them I think the local health and safety officer would have had a bit of a field day. There seemed to be a lot of short cuts taken but the thing that got me was that if I wanted to move there, I couldn't buy a property – they were only available to rent for foreigners. Admittedly the rent was respectable, about $1,000 US (£650) a month for a decent apartment, although you could perhaps find something cheaper if you shopped around.

It was quite reasonable really – but it's not Essex, is it!

Towards the end of our stay, we were taken to a nature reserve, where it had been arranged for us all to have an elephant ride. That's not something you do every day, is it? I'd thoroughly recommend it, though; we went on a trek around the fields and through the woods and it was so exhilarating. They are magnificent animals with such a gentle disposition and it was properly relaxing. Not that I can remember that far back but it felt like you were being rocked in your cot by your mum.

As the others were getting ready to say their goodbyes, I was making plans to welcome a visitor. Marie came out and we stayed on for another ten days after everyone else had left and had a little holiday. We thoroughly enjoyed it and could see the attraction of retiring to the sun, but agreed that India, at that time, wasn't right for us.

The Real Marigold Hotel was screened across three episodes and was originally shown on BBC2. The series was universally acclaimed and nominated for a BAFTA and won an online British Broadcasting award – which was presented by Jonathan Ross – plus other international factual documentary awards. No surprise then that it was re-commissioned and bumped on to the larger audience of BBC1. Over the course of the next two or three years the original crew were joined by other celebrities 'of a certain age' and were taken to other parts of the globe. Along with Miriam, Wayne and Rosemary, I sampled life in Florida, Kyoto in Japan and Chengdu in China, whilst Jan Leeming joined Miriam, Wayne and me in Cuba's capital, Havana.

Other celebrities did episodes in such far-flung places as Buenos Aires, Reykjavik, Thailand, Vietnam and Mexico, whilst I was back on board for a trip to St Petersburg in Russia, along with Miriam, former Three Degrees singer Sheila Ferguson and the former politician Stanley Johnson, father of ex-prime minister Boris.

I'll tell you all about those adventures a little bit later on.

COME DINE WITH ME

ANOTHER DAYTIME television show that I was invited to appear on was a celebrity version of *Come Dine With Me*, the programme where five people take it in turns to host and cook for the others. The guests give their marks each day and at the end of the week there's an overall winner.

It's actually recorded over five weeks, a separate episode each week.

I was told that I was to be the first host, which meant that I had no idea who any of the other guests would be. On the day of the hosting Marie put herself on look-out, waiting to see who would arrive, although she knew who the others were but was sworn to secrecy from me. Not that I would know any of them anyway!

First to the door was Pete Burns. You may know who Pete Burns was: I didn't. On answering the door I was immediately confronted by the sight of my first guest wearing a skirt and full make-up.

I couldn't stop myself saying, 'Fucking hell!'

Honestly, I had no idea who he was and after a few nervous moments, the production team stepped in, introduced me to the lead singer from the group Dead or Alive and then asked if we could re-record his arrival.

The show had got off to a less than ideal start.

Next to come knocking was Andrew Stone, a dancer. He immediately thrust his leg up on my shoulder and asked if I could do that.

'What the fuck would I want to do that for?' I said.

The other guests were Chantelle Houghton, who I also didn't know and Cleo Rocos, who I hadn't seen since she used to be on *The Kenny Everett Show* in the 1980s.

It had all the makings of an awkward evening, which is probably what the production team were after. We had a drink and then went outside. I've got an outdoor kitchen that I use for cooking Chinese food; it's called 'Wok This Way'.

My overall culinary skills aren't too bad but my preference is always to do a Chinese meal, so I'd given it all some careful thought and decided to go with spare ribs as a starter, then a nice chicken chow mein, special fried rice and curry sauce with lychees and cream to finish.

As soon as they saw the menu I could hear the whispering, 'I bet he's ordered a takeaway' and that sort of stuff, so I had to show them my kitchen and preparation area. Some of them also believed that I'd hired the place for the evening, so I ended up giving them a guided tour of George Hall just to convince them that we really lived there.

Pete Burns asked for some tea and just sat there drinking it, with cigarette in hand and generally just cut himself off from the others. When he saw the menu he complained that he didn't like spare ribs, yet scoffed the lot when I served them up. In fact, there wasn't a clean plate to be seen anywhere and everyone seemed to have had a good time.

If you remember the programme, the diners were then filmed in a taxi, supposedly on their way home, talking about the evening and giving their marks out of ten. In truth, they just took them for a short ride up my drive and then brought them back.

This process seemed to take forever and then there was some sort of discussion going on amongst the crew. I was told, in confidence, that everyone had given me top marks and that I couldn't be beaten. This wasn't what they wanted from the first show; they wanted a bit of jeopardy about who would go on and win. One or two of the guests were then asked to re-do their marks. What a con. This went on until about two in the morning before they'd got what they wanted. Over the next few weeks the others took turns in hosting and we got to know each other a little better before the grand reveal at the end, where they announced Cleo and Pete as the overall joint-winners and me second!

Another foodie-type show I did was called *Who's Doing the Dishes*, presented by Brian McFadden. The idea was that some members of the general public came to the house, were given a meal and if they guessed their host (in this instance, me!) then I would have to do the washing-up. If they couldn't then they would be left with a kitchen full of pots.

In reality, the production team cleared it all up anyway but they must have been the thickest bunch around because the panel couldn't identify me from all the clues.

It was a little bit like *Through the Keyhole*, something else I've done. Anyway, the clues couldn't have been any easier. I put lots of different darts photographs all around, including a big one of Eric Bristow in the bedroom. We had my candelabras, cloaks and gold on display. I was in a different room but could see them on a monitor. 'Do you think it could be Elton John?' said one. Another thought it could be the home of Sharon and Ozzy Osbourne. Really?

Then they started to get my back up, saying things like, 'it's a bit dated', and 'look at those old-fashioned chandeliers'. One even said they didn't like the colour scheme of the house.

Despite all the clues it was obvious that none of them had the foggiest idea whose house they were in, so even more hints were dropped in their direction.

'The name George is prominent ...'

'Both father and son are darts players.'

Nothing, the thick gits.

The programme finished and in theory they were supposed to then go and do the washing-up but that bit was skipped for some reason. At this point, some 20 minutes after they'd finished, one bloke suddenly said, 'Is it Bobby George?'

They thought about re-doing the ending but by now it was nearly three in the morning and Brian McFadden had been stretched out on the sofa for over an hour. I said I wouldn't re-do the outcome and told them to clear off, I'd had enough by then. Pointedly, I also mentioned to the contestants that I would be getting the decorators in as the colour scheme hadn't met with their approval!

Another programme I was involved in was called *Poker Academy* and had been put together by Mike Reid, he of *The Comedians* and *EastEnders* fame. I'd known Mike on and off for many years as he used to do the pubs around my area when I first started playing. He'd be in there giving it the full patter on a Saturday or Sunday afternoon.

I used to enjoy chatting to him but it could take forever to have a conversation as he'd be concentrating on doing his roll-ups whilst he was telling you a story. Golden Virginia, that was his thing, all very precisely done.

They wanted me to play a doorman in a short film he was making about how to play poker. A company from Hollywood were behind it apparently, so I didn't take a great deal of persuading.

They told me to be at the London Dungeons to do the filming, which raised a few doubts, but it was done out beautifully with posh carpets and elegant chandeliers and we had a good couple of days filming there. I liked Mike, another decent fella gone far too soon.

Apart from the telly stuff I occasionally get an invitation that looks too good to be true. A number of years ago Marie and I were invited to go on a cruise, all expenses paid. Now I happen to fancy myself living a life on the ocean wave. All I had to do was a couple of question-and-answer sessions for the guests, you know the sort of thing: 'An Audience with Bobby George'. Easy peasy and very good fun, except the bloomin' cruise was for two weeks around the Baltic Sea. It was July but it felt like the middle of winter!

Cold doesn't even begin to describe it and bobbing about between the icebergs you can't exactly just say that you've had enough and want to get off. It was really rough and Marie was constantly seasick, so we couldn't wait for it to end. Somehow, we managed to stick it out and I dropped a few subtle hints that I'd do it again but it would have to be a Caribbean cruise next time. Funnily enough, we haven't heard back from them yet!

MARIGOLDS, STATESIDE

FOLLOWING OUR experiences in India, Miriam Margolyes, Wayne Sleep, Rosemary Shrager and I were eager to continue our *Marigold* adventure and were invited to go to Florida to discover how senior citizens make the most of their retirement in America.

We flew to Orlando and were transported to a place called Oak Run, a gated community for up to 7,000 elderly residents. It didn't take long to see the attraction of living there: lovely warm weather and lots of healthy activities to take part in and clubs to join.

On the first morning, Miriam and Wayne took part in the aerobics, whilst Rosemary and I showed willing by having a go at the Pilates in the ballroom. The gentle exercise was clearly beneficial; my usual morning routine generally involves nothing more strenuous than swallowing that many tablets you can hear me rattle.

One of the things we were eager to discover the truth about was the notion that anyone can walk into a shop in America and buy a gun. They took me and Miriam down to a local gun shop but we ran into cultural difficulties almost as soon as we got inside. We'd barely had time to say hello before Miriam was in trouble. It was around that time that Donald Trump was running for president for the first time and there were signs of support everywhere in the shop.

'Vote for Trump' the posters said, with Florida being one of his key states. Miriam isn't renowned for her tact: 'Are all you fucking arseholes going to vote for Trump?' was her opener.

I told her to be careful what she was saying; after all, we were in a gun shop in a country where some folk have very itchy trigger fingers. 'They're all fucking arseholes,' she went on, undeterred.

I feared that it wouldn't be too long before she was asked to leave the premises and take her opinions elsewhere. We were told that nearly every resident of Oak Run owns a weapon of some sort, at which point Miriam was given a gun to hold.

'I don't like guns, I don't want one and I don't approve of them,' she stated.

We'd made such a good impression by this stage that I was relieved when the shop owner asked if we fancied going on the range to fire some weapons. 'It's only up the road,' he said.

I thought I'd have some of that, so agreed to go with him. Rosemary and Wayne joined us but Miriam declined the invitation. Only up the road!! It took us an hour and a half to get there. But I suppose in a country of that size it was only up the road.

Once we'd arrived we were shown around the premises and Rosemary was handed a gun to hold but was immediately told off.

'Madam, please don't point that gun at me,' said the startled shop attendant. 'You never point a gun at anyone because you can never be sure if it's loaded or not.'

We then went to the indoor shooting range, where they let us try out a variety of weapons, with some of the high-powered ones firing off ten rounds per second.

I've legally owned guns for much of my adult life and am used to firing them but this was something else. It certainly wasn't easy, as some of our party discovered, spraying rounds all over the place.

Shooting is seen as something of a hobby for many Americans; as soon as they're old enough they go to a range and learn how to fire a gun. Contrary to popular beliefs, though, we were told that it isn't that easy for people to just go out and buy one. They do carry out background checks on any individual wanting to purchase a firearm, although it's quite a speedy process, a couple of weeks for a rifle and up to a month for a handgun. Different states have different firearm laws, but it was a little comforting to know you can't just buy one off the shelf and go out and shoot someone. In times of war, there's certainly enough people that could be called up, though; nearly everyone we spoke to claimed to own a gun and knew how to fire it.

From what I could see, that is never going to be changed and guns aren't ever going to be banned as their Constitution gives them the right to carry and use firearms. It's part of their heritage and goes back to the olden days; firearms have always ruled the Wild West.

For the final few days of our Florida visit we relocated to Palm Beach County, staying at the exclusive Polo Club resort. My word – hello – this place really was the ultimate in top-end retirement living. We were shown to our digs and were pleasantly surprised to find out that we were to be accommodated in a luxurious $2.5 million villa.

There were so many cushions and pillows on my bed I had to remove about a dozen of them to get in. I couldn't give a monkeys about luxury really, it doesn't mean a thing to me, in fact everything was all rather too la-di-da pretentious for moi.

Our stay there was timed nicely because it coincided with a glamorous shindig that had been arranged for the rich and famous. Over 800 people were there, with many of them being golfers and tennis players; they all seemed to know each other and all were stinking rich. There was something striking that linked them all; looking around the room I thought I was at a cosmetic surgery convention. All of them appeared to have had treatment of some sort and it's impossible to imagine how many pulls and tucks had been done across the room.

Most looked ridiculous, with their skin pulled tightly up and every time they opened their gob you could see rows of pearly white teeth. Eavesdropping on conversations, you could sense the only thing they were interested in was how many material things they owned. One woman came up to me and looked at my Rolex watch and gold rings. 'You must be a millionaire,' she said, as if accepting me into her inner circle. 'I'm not – but my wife is,' I laughed.

As I've already said, I thought the various procedures made most of them look awful but one of our number was clearly interested in finding out more. Rosemary told us that she was thinking about trying Botox, possibly having a couple of fillers around her eyes. She told us that it might cost up to $1,000 but that she was more than happy to pay up if it helped to remove some of the lines on her face. Unable to help myself, I suggested that it might cost a lot more than $1,000 to do that!

I don't think she knew if I was joking or not when I said it and battle lines were drawn again later, when she returned from seeing a specialist.

'When are you going to have it done then, doll?' I asked her, chuckling to myself.

'Oh Bobby,' she wailed. 'I've had it done!'

'Really?' I enquired. 'It doesn't look any different. Can't you ask for your money back?'

I don't think she appreciated my sense of humour but each to their own. It seemed like a waste of money to me and not something you'll ever see me doing.

PARPING IN OSAKA

IT WASN'T too long before the *Marigold* crew were off on our travels again, this time to Japan, a country I've always longed to visit but had never got round to it. Now I was doing it with my new group of friends: Miriam, Wayne and Rosemary. We flew to Osaka, then got a train to Kyoto and our arrival coincided with the height of the monsoon season; I've never seen so much rain in all my life.

Our digs for the week were with 73-year-old twin sisters, who were so polite, bowing all the time to us. We must have represented a strange intrusion into their lives. Miriam farts on a regular basis and there's never any attempt to conceal it, even in the most refined company. Parp, parp. Wayne is naturally flamboyant and won't miss any opportunity to show off his theatrics, whilst Rosemary shouts all the time and barks like a dog. I've not the foggiest idea what they made of the fourth member of our group though!

We'd not been inside their home for five minutes before the girls were arguing over the rooms. They didn't really get on with regards to things like that: 'I want that room,' 'No, I want that room!' Who gives a fuck? As long as our Japanese hosts didn't expect me to sleep on the floor, like they did, then I couldn't have cared less. If I'd wanted a pee in the middle of the night I would never have got up.

Most senior citizens go to their local park in the morning to exercise to a routine that is transmitted on national radio at 6.30 every day. The locals enthusiastically engaged in it and tolerated our presence with quizzical looks. It's probably fair to say that Wayne was the only one of our group that got anything out of it.

Japan is keen for their elderly to remain active and contribute to society, so there is a system in place called the Silver Human Resource Centre, which sources jobs for the over-60s. There are 1,200 branches across Japan and there are 5,000 employed in Kyoto alone. The four of us went to be interviewed and were given roles within the local community: Rosemary and Wayne were assigned jobs in a nearby restaurant, whilst Miriam and I were sent to work as sales assistants in a gift shop. It was quite a long walk from where we were staying to reach the gift shop and I was still waiting for my knee operation, so couldn't make it without help. Surprisingly, that help came from Miriam, who herself needed a new knee. We got hold of a wheelchair and she was able to push me, leaning on it as we went.

A couple of days beforehand I'd seen a Ready Mix concrete lorry on the road and couldn't believe how new and shiny it looked. It had chrome bumpers, chrome wheels, clean paintwork and windows and was absolutely spotless. I presumed it must be off to a show somewhere. As Miriam pushed me, we went past a building site and there were loads of these lorries all lined up, all in pristine condition. We got closer and you couldn't see any concrete on any of them anywhere, they all looked brand new. I asked about it and was told that the drivers are given a new lorry at the start of their employment and have to keep them looking like that. Whilst they are waiting to load or unload, they are continually cleaning them.

It's the same with the cars; no one drives a dirty car in Japan, society is geared towards cleanliness and it just didn't appear to be in anyone's nature to leave anything dirty or to drop litter. Smokers are conscious of disposing of their cigarettes and matches properly and when anyone buys any chewing gum they're also given a little purse to pop it in afterwards before chucking it in a bin. In that regard, I think there's plenty that we could learn from them.

Kitted out in our uniforms, we tried our best in the gift shop but the language differences didn't help. Sporting my best smile at all times I greeted every customer that came into the shop with a courteous bow. How the Japanese love to bow – it did my nut in to be honest but when in Rome … or Kyoto!

My retail skills were found to be totally inadequate as I don't think we sold a thing and those few hours were mainly spent bowing and pointing at things, and Miriam didn't fare any better either. It made for some light entertainment for the television programme we were there to make but apart from that, it was an afternoon of my life that I'll never get back!

We rounded off our trip with a visit to an authentic Buddhist temple where, if you drank the natural spring water, it increased your life expectancy. I glugged some down in the hope that I'll live for another 60 years. The older I get, the happier I am that I didn't die young; in fact the only time I feel old is when I look in a mirror.

We'd travelled there on one of the famed bullet trains, which really are as incredible as everyone makes out. It's probably more like taking a flight than train travel and the punctuality is unbelievable. You line up on the platform and if it says it will arrive at nine minutes and two seconds past the hour, you can guarantee it will. Once you are on board, they come and offer you some tea or coffee and then away you go. Very efficient, very regimented, very impressive.

Overall, I enjoyed Japan – except for the food. I couldn't do that, no way. I thought it was fucking awful actually. In the western world we will get a Japanese or Chinese take-away meal or go to a restaurant and think the food is delicious. The truth is, it's made for our palate and tastes nothing like it does in its homeland. Generally, I'm not a fussy eater but I couldn't take all the grasses and berries and everything else they wanted me to try. I'd have probably made more of an effort if I was starving but for a few days I was comfortably able to get by on a few bowls of Kellogg's Corn Flakes and some Mars Bars.

The rest of our small party put on a brave face at meal times, 'Oh this is lovely, this is marvellous.' Bullshitters!

Arigato Japan, Sayonara.

PANDA-ING FOR EFFECT

HAVING SURVIVED a few days getting to know Japan, alongside Wayne, Rosemary and Miriam, I saw no reason not to agree to a similar-style adventure to China with them. For the next *Marigold* trip the four musketeers were reunited in Chengdu, capital of Sichuan province, a place that had been voted the country's happiest place in which to live and is also the home of the giant panda.

Wayne, Rosemary and I flew together from the UK, whilst Miriam joined us in the world's most populated nation after flying in from Hollywood, where she'd been filming. We stayed in the home of our host, Vicky, but were left to our own devices, which was always going to be an issue. Wandering out on the first evening, the fact that we were way off a traditional tourist spot couldn't have been more obvious. There were no direction signs that we could comprehend and no one around who could speak any English to help us.

Finding a restaurant was no help either, a lot of pointing and miming only resulted in us receiving the most bland, tasteless dishes. As Wayne said, understating things somewhat, 'This really is a baptism of fire.' The local cuisine certainly wasn't going to be to my liking and thankfully Rosemary did the majority of the cooking from then on.

Naturally, we were encouraged to participate in local events for the elderly and that meant an early start when we went down to the local park to join in with their morning rituals. It's normal practice for senior citizens to go and participate in a communal singing and dancing session. The group had one or two who could speak English and they told us they dance every morning to keep fit and find joy. I'm not sure who Joy was but I do hope they managed to find her …

After the activity, they all like a cup of tea together and invited us to join them at one of the traditional tea houses. We all know the old saying 'for all the tea in China', so I was looking forward to sampling it. What a disappointment it was; it wasn't nice at all, really bitter. Knowing we were all on camera as we tasted it, Miriam and Rosemary went, 'Oh, that's absolutely wonderful.'

I couldn't disguise my thoughts as well as they did.

'Fucking hell, that's awful,' I said. 'Not my cup of tea at all!'

I did enjoy walking through the parks there, learning about the different trees and admiring all the water features and the wonderful ponds full of fish. But there's no doubt that we were all looking forward very much to one special feature on our itinerary, the day we were to head out into the countryside to see the giant pandas.

The high-speed rail network is relatively cheap, costing around £2 for the 34-mile, 20-minute ride to Du Jiang Yan, a 400 square mile regional reserve dedicated to the preservation of the giant panda. The facility rescues sick and injured pandas and operates a vitally important breeding programme. At the time of our visit there were just 1,864 pandas left in the wild, with another 500 kept in captivity.

This place looked after pandas, nurtured them back to full health and let them go back out into the wild. These precious animals are so vulnerable to infectious diseases we had to put on protective clothing before we were allowed in and were all suited up like spacemen as we approached them.

I'd never imagined that I would be able to get so close to these wonderful creatures but the experience brought out different emotions amongst the four of us. Miriam was soon in tears because they were all behind bars.

When you look at a photograph of a panda or see them on television they look lovely, don't they? All beautiful pure black and white fur. But when you get up close to them the white isn't very clean at all, it looks like someone has pissed all over them.

Don't be fooled by the cuddly appearance either, they've got razor-sharp four- or five-inch-long claws. Before we went in to see them, one of the keepers told us about one of his former colleagues at the facility. A female panda had experienced a difficult birth and was understandably very protective of the new arrival. The next morning the keeper could see the mother but was unable to locate the baby and was concerned. He went in to have a closer inspection and the mother went for him aggressively and ripped off one of his arms with just one swipe. Other keepers quickly rushed to the scene to give help and their actions saved the poor man's life. Surgeons were able to sew his arm back on and give him full use of it, although he was hospitalised for around nine months.

It's a bit of a myth that giant pandas only eat bamboo as well. That is their staple diet admittedly, and it's not any old bamboo either, it needs to be a certain type which they'll happily devour for up to 16 hours a day. But they love a carrot, absolutely love them and I was able to sit for half an hour feeding carrots through the cage to one particular panda who decided he was happy to share a bit of bonding time with me.

It's a day I'll never forget and I hope that the facility continues to look after and nurture these wonderful creatures for many more generations to come.

CUBAN HEELS

MY NEXT *Marigold* adventure was to another part of the world that I'd never visited before, the sunny Caribbean island of Cuba, alongside regular travel companions Miriam and Wayne, plus former newsreader Jan Leeming.

We'd heard all about the island's reputation before landing and our first impressions backed it up. It really is like going back in time and that feeling was enforced as we were driven from the airport to our accommodation in Havana in a 1949 Chevy. Ours wasn't the only old jalopy either, we saw hundreds of retro American vehicles on the roads and the stench of petrol fumes in the air was horrendous.

If you're not looking at the cars then you need to keep an eye on the architecture in Havana. Many of the buildings have either fallen down or are close to ruin, whilst many of those standing have been daubed with large murals of Che Guevara.

We were split into pairs and a lovely couple called Horacio and Marta had kindly agreed to have Miriam and I stay with them. They were wonderful and couldn't have been more hospitable but, as ever, I'm not too sure what they made of my little mate Miriam and her eccentric ways.

Horacio and Marta told us everything we needed to know about the island and we learned that there is still an element of state control in Cuba, particularly with things like the internet, which is amongst the most tightly controlled in the world. For the vast majority of the population home connection is totally banned, so to use it you must go to your local Wi-Fi zone, which for us happened to be in the middle of a nearby park. As always, our brief was to gauge what life was like for the senior citizen and we were shocked to find that the state pension is as low as $11 a month. With Wi-Fi access costing around $1.50 an hour, surfing the net doesn't come cheap for your average Cuban. The procedure for getting online is fairly simple though: you buy a scratch card and away you go. Miriam decided she needed to keep up to speed with her emails, so we sat one morning while she worked her way through about 150 of them.

I couldn't care less about anything like that. Back home, Marie looks after any work stuff that comes my way, so I found myself free to natter to a few of the locals in the park. The first chap I spoke to made me think of Alan Evans, my old Welsh darts mate, because he told me that he made Cuban heels for a living. Short of stature, Alan loved a Cuban heel. I always used to tease him that he needed a pair of steps to get in them!

My new pal seemed happy to chat and told me all about the Fidel Castro days and how he was always fearful of being caught listening to his favourite band – The Beatles. Under the communist regime it was forbidden for anyone on the island to listen to music of that sort, he told me. And anyone who was caught would face some time in detention. My friend was resourceful; he made a record player whilst at university and went down into his cellar each evening to listen to some of The Beatles records that he'd managed to source from somewhere. The irony is that in the same park that we were sat in, there now stands a statue of John Lennon. As a nation, the Cubans loved the music of The Beatles yet weren't allowed to listen to it. How stupid is that?

He also told me how difficult it is to get paint there. You just can't get it on the island and if you are able to source some, absolutely none is wasted, they even get a rag and wipe around the rim of the can to use every drop. There are lots of brightly coloured buildings in Havana, pinks, yellows and greens everywhere, but it's not to make the place look like a summer garden; it's because they have to use what they can get. In most instances they don't bother, so many of the buildings are in disrepair, run down and rotting.

When Castro took over, there were many who wanted to get out of the country and go to the United States, so they were given money but had to surrender their homes to the state. Spanish-built, these properties were magnificent in their day, with granite columns, gothic arches and sweeping staircases but they are all falling to bits now and it made me feel ill to look at them. Any metal surfaces have long since rusted over and telegraph wires are hanging limply from every pole; it looks like the bomb has dropped in some areas.

Although the state pension is very low in Cuba, locals manage to get by because there are two different price structures on the island: one for them and one for tourists. Something might seem quite expensive to a visitor but be reasonably priced for a resident.

The sun shone brightly throughout our stay and in a warm climate there's a natural tendency to spend more time outside and every pavement had tables of elderly gents playing dominoes. One group invited me to join them for a beer and a few games and I had a bit of good fortune by beating the local champ. I enjoyed seeing the pleasure they were getting from such a simple and inexpensive game and if nothing else I kept them on their toes for a while before local honour was restored.

I very much enjoyed Cuba and think it has lots going for it. They have some of the best medical facilities, doctors and surgeons in the world and have one of the highest life expectancy rates in Latin America.

Of all the places we went to on our *Marigold* trips, Cuba is certainly one to consider if you're looking for a sun-drenched place in which to spend your golden years. Wayne, in particular, loved it. They have a culture that is strongly geared towards dance, so he was in his element and there were so many places he could go and express himself – dancing and prancing I called it. 'Come on darling, it's time to go,' I'd say to him and he would pretend to be under my thumb and make a big thing about wanting to stay.

WINMAU

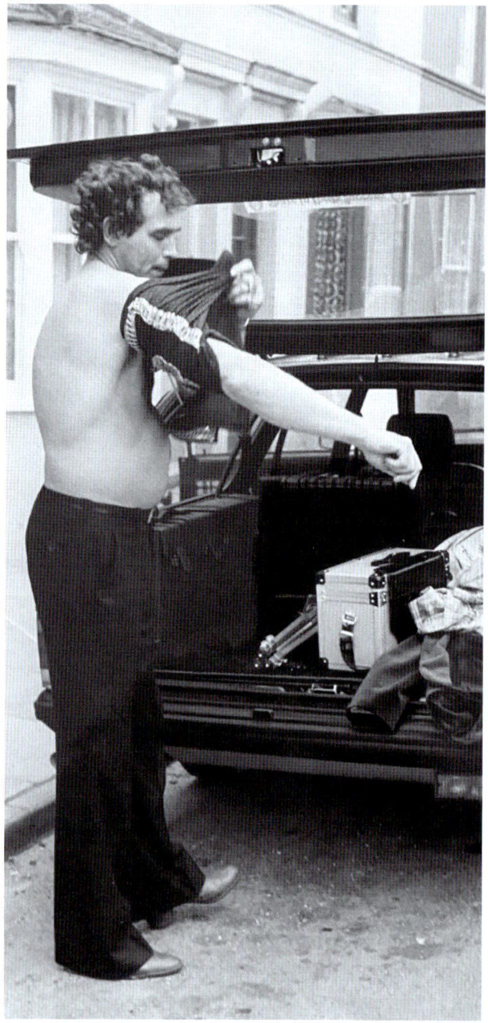

I was never afraid to graft but always left enough time for a quick shirt change and then off to do an exhibition.

The hardest of them all to win – my two News of the World *titles, with actress Diana Dors and glamour model Maria Whittaker making the presentations.*

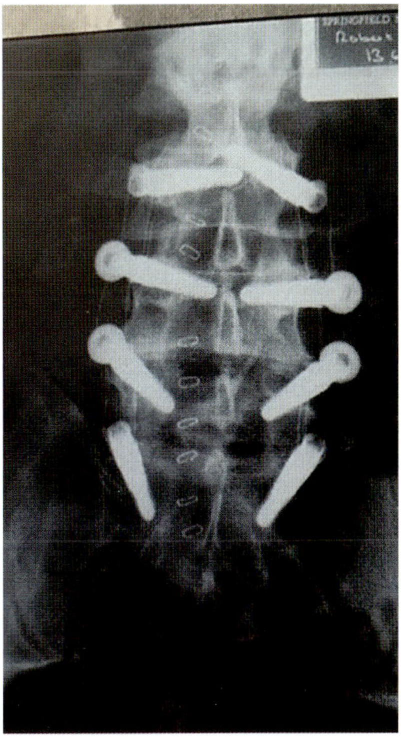

'An hour away from death,' so grateful for the nurses who helped me recover from a ruptured spleen (1981)

Pinning my hopes on a full recovery, eight titanium screws were inserted to hold my back together (1994)

George Hall. Can he build it? Yes he can!

Tweety Pie and Mrs Claus, practically part of the family

My old friend Lance Hardy RIP

Brother Kevin, we value our time together more and more these days.

Man of the Match on England duty, the day we beat Scotland 12-0

Signing a few autographs alongside Maureen Flowers.

Some of my old mates, with Alan Glazier

Eric Bristow

Tony Sontag

Jocky Wilson

Paul Booth has worked as the MC for Eric and I for years and was with the great man when he died.

Laughs are never far away when you're with Little Richard Ashdown

Dressed to kill, Paul Booth, the James Bond of darts

I had my chances in the 1980 World Final but it didn't affect my relationship with Eric.

Marie on 14 February 1984, the day I met her and told her I was going to marry her!

GRUMBLE AND GRUNT AND VLADIMIR PUTIN

OUR NEXT adventure was in St Petersburg in Russia, where my companions were politician Stanley Johnson, singer Sheila Ferguson, of Three Degrees fame, plus my old mate Miriam.

St Petersburg is a city with a rich cultural heritage and is known as the 'Venice of the North' on account of the stunning waterways. Upon arrival they gave Miriam and me a mobility scooter apiece to get around on. They were both the same, yet the Harry Potter actor wasn't happy: she complained like mad that mine went faster than hers.

I'd not met Stanley before, so we decided to go and have a few drinks to get to know each other a little better. The local beer was around four times cheaper than ours, so it would have been a waste not to try a few while we were there.

I'm not sure Stanley had ever come across Cockney rhyming slang in the past, so asked me to go through a few little sayings with him. He was so fascinated by my use of the English language that he whipped out a notebook and pencil to write down some of the better ones:

Pig's ear – beer

Laugh and a joke – smoke

Winkle bag – fag

Blow about – snout

He was lapping it up and knew that I was teasing him when I said, 'Ere, the grumble and grunt isn't very good here, is it?'

'Grumble and grunt, what do you mean, Robert?' he replied, quizzically.

I couldn't help but laugh. 'You know Stanley, you know, the old Jack and Danny!'

It took an age for the penny to drop and he just smiled and said, 'I think it's time for another pig's ear!'

We did and then we had another one and another one. You couldn't tell we were in a communist country; all the familiar British brands were available on tap, and we'd sampled a few of them before he then came back with a couple of vodkas.

'It's the national drink in Russia, Bobby, we've got to try it,' he said. 'Down in one hit.'

So, I just went boom, downing it in one go. He looked amazed and asked how I'd done that. 'It's nothing,' I told him. 'I'm a beer drinker, so that's not a problem.'

He eyed me suspiciously then downed his in one go, spluttering as it hit the sweet spot. We had a couple more each in quick succession and I could tell that he was merrily on his way to being pissed.

Stanley and I are from different – very different – walks of life. He is all toodaloo pip pip, pass the moo-tard old boy, whilst I'm a bit rougher round the edges but we found common ground that evening in St Petersburg and quietly got hammered together.

During our stay there, we went to a naval parade on the banks of the river Neva. The city turned out in huge numbers to witness the show of Russia's military power, with over 40 warships and submarines on display. Overhead, the country's aerobatic team performed a Red Arrows-type flyover, with coloured vapour trails filling the sky.

Word spread amongst the onlookers that President Putin would be in attendance, out of harm's way on his motor launch in the middle of the river.

'Was Putin in the navy?' Sheila asked a local woman.

'No,' she replied, icily. 'Just the KGB.'

The might of the Russian navy made its way up this big, wide river and then we saw the president's launch at the rear of the cavalcade. Stanley mentioned that he'd actually met Putin on official business, when he'd been here for a meeting five years earlier. It didn't look as if the Russian president was keen on renewing relationships as he sped by, although he did wave in our direction.

'See that?' I said. 'He's just said to his buddy, "Isn't that Bobby George over there?"'

Putin hails from St Petersburg and we were shown the estate and the block of flats that he grew up in. It was a bit of a shithole really; he clearly didn't come from money but certainly has plenty of it now.

Fancying a feed one day, Miriam and I decided to go out and have lunch together. We found a fairly modest café and had the steak and chips. Lovely it was, Miriam couldn't get over the chips and it only cost about a fiver each. The next time we went out we found ourselves in a slightly posher place and we ordered the same, steak and chips. Once more, it was delicious and Miriam was again left eulogising about the chips, even though it was about £8 each this time.

When we had steak and chips for the third time in the week we were actually in a very posh restaurant, chandeliers, the lot. The food was equally delicious but good value, even though it came to about £15 this time.

'I can't get over the chips in this country, they're the best I've ever tasted,' Miriam announced. I told her that I thought they were OK as well but not quite as fantastic as she was making out. 'They've only peeled the potatoes and dropped them in the fryer,' I told her.

'You mean they're not frozen?' was her response.

It transpired that Miriam only ever eats frozen chips, she wouldn't dream of taking a potato and peeling it. Her taste buds were doing overtime simply because she was eating fresh chips! Incredible.

After several days in St Petersburg we thanked our host Irina for her hospitality and travelled around 200 miles south where we were to spend our final days in Russia discovering the restorative benefits of a traditional health farm. The sanatorium was basically a spa and retreat for the elderly. We were medically questioned and examined and offered various remedies and treatments that they thought might be good for us.

I tried something called a dry carbonic bath, which they said passed carbon dioxide into my skin, which then changed into oxygen. If that sounds radical it was nothing to what Miriam got up to. Firstly, she scoffed a whole raw onion then it was recommended to her that she allow some leeches to be put on her skin – supposedly they can help your blood flow better.

I whispered quietly to the camera, 'They'll need a fucking lot of leeches to treat her!' Fair play to her though, she tried it and said she felt the benefits afterwards. I could only imagine how the poor leeches were feeling!

Miriam was always on at me to talk properly – 'Enunciate your words Bobby,' she'd say. 'Open your mouth wide when you talk because I can't understand a word you are saying.'

So, I'd ham it up and exaggerate, just for a giggle, 'Oh, hellllllllooooooo Miriam, how the very devil are youuuuuuu this morning?'

I'd like to think that Miriam and I have been to so many places together now that we totally get each other and have formed a bond that will always be there. Certainly, there's not much we don't know about each other and it's probably fair to say that my old mate isn't shy when it comes to wandering in and out of some of the bathrooms we've shared together. There's a thought for you to conjure with!

When we weren't taking the mickey out of each other we were supposed to be finding out how senior citizens live in Russia, as opposed to other parts of the world. We discovered that they have an interesting system there; when a citizen reaches retirement age they are given a flat, normally somewhere up at the top of a high tower block. They still receive a state pension, but all their heating and lighting bills are automatically taken care of. It seems like a decent way of doing things, provided the lifts work!

When sharing life experiences with some of the elderly in Russia I had to agree with what one chap said to me, 'When you get older, time goes quicker. It makes you appreciate life and if you do that you'll live for another day.'

He was bang on. I remember watching a television programme once where a tree in a desert somewhere lives for about 11,000 years. Others might not fancy it but that would do for me; I certainly wouldn't mind being that tree. Whenever anyone asks me if I've got any unfulfilled ambitions left I always tell them it's to live a long while!

SO LONG OLD PALS

ERIC BRISTOW'S death hit me hard. He was only 60 for fuck's sake and that's no age these days, is it? I'd known him since he was a teenager and he never changed: a precocious cocky Cockney, who took the darts world by storm and went on to win five world titles, beating me in one of the most talked-about finals of all time. He could be a pain in the arse and we had some right ding-dongs over the years but for most of the time he was my mate and we had some great times together.

Fate decreed that I'd see him just before he left us but I still can't get over how strangely the events of that sad day panned out.

The Premier League has become big business and if you've been to one of the events or even just been in one of the hosting cities you'll be aware that darts fans come from far and wide to make the most of the occasion. As a prelude to the evening's events, myself and Eric used to get the punters in the mood beforehand. There's a Shooters Bar and Diner within the vicinity of many of the host venues and it became a regular booking for me to do an exhibition in there between 2pm and 5pm and then Eric would do the VIP meet and greet stuff from

5pm to 7pm. It was a steady little earner for us both and good for any darts fan who wanted to get on the pop nice and early.

On 5 April 2018 I was at the Shooters Bar in Liverpool, just across from the Echo Arena and was doing my stuff with Paul Booth as my MC. The crowd built steadily throughout the afternoon and the banter was top-notch, as it usually is in Liverpool. They're a great crowd up there. Just before the end of the afternoon Eric popped in to say hello, before he started his stint at the arena. We had a little catch-up and I got him a Guinness and then made my excuses as I had to go on to another event.

'Go well son,' I told him. 'See you when you're older.' That's a normal thing I'd say to a mate when parting. Sadly I didn't see him again.

I was due to be working in Stoke-on-Trent the next day and had agreed to stay at a pub run by Barry Birch, who used to be Eric's driver. Barry sometimes came to George Hall to do a spot of fishing and when I told him that I was coming to Stoke he offered me the use of one of his spare rooms for the night. 'Come and stay with me Bob, we'll have a right old catch-up,' he said.

I had a steady journey down the M6 and a couple of hours after leaving Liverpool I was having a cup of tea with Barry in the lounge above his pub. Obviously, Eric was soon mentioned and I said, 'He lives near here, doesn't he?' A Londoner by birth, Eric had moved to Stoke in the late 1970s, when he was in a relationship with Maureen Flowers, and had settled in the area for the rest of his life.

Barry led me to his kitchen window and pointed across, to where Eric's flat was, less than 200 yards away from where we were standing. I'd been to his flat once, about ten years earlier and was gazing towards it when my phone rang.

I could see it was Paul Booth calling.

'Hello Paul?' how's things' I said.

'I've got some bad news Bobby,' he began. 'Eric's dead. We were just outside in the car park, Eric was rolling a fag and then he just hit the floor, dead.'

I couldn't believe the suddenness of his passing, nor could I take in the fact that I could see his flat – the same flat he'd have left just a few hours earlier – as I was trying to take in the tragic news. What were the odds of it: me being with him, saying goodbye, going to Stoke and looking out of a window at his flat whilst stood alongside his former driver?

We both needed a stiff drink that night.

They reckon Eric's heart must have stopped before he hit the ground as there was no blood. In his diary, apparently, he'd written that he'd got bad chest pains. Bloody hell, if that was the case why didn't he go to the doctors or the hospital and get it sorted?

Knowing Eric he probably thought, 'I'll put loads of Guinness down my neck, that'll get rid of the pain.'

Anyone who knew him was aware that he didn't exactly lead a healthy lifestyle. For as long as I'd known him he was a heavy smoker, always rolling his own and he'd think nothing of getting through 15 or 16 pints of Guinness in a day and rounding it all off with a curry. Nobody's body can handle that day in, day out. Always on the go, working and travelling, meant he was always pushing it, although it wasn't work to him, just a chance to get on the piss every day.

I like a drink and a smoke but there are extremes and Eric pushed them to the limit. 'You smoke too much and you drink too much,' I'd say to him.

'I know all about that Bob,' he'd start. 'But put it this way, no one is going to be pushing me around in a wheelchair; when I go, I'll go like that. Bang.'

And he fucking did as well, bang.

It was only three months later that I lost another of my closest darts chums, Tony Sontag. A gentle, caring soul, we had some great times together and I was devastated when I heard that cancer had returned and taken him at such a young age.

I used to call him the Cheshire Cat because he had a big, broad, beaming smile and that's how I'll always remember him. Tony was a proper wind-up merchant but was also a terrific player, who first made his name as one of the stars of a really strong London County side in the late 1970s. He had good runs to the semi-finals of both the British Open and the World Masters to kick-start his darts career, which he combined with his own roofing business.

Lifting the BBC Bullseye Trophy, a one-off competition that featured all the top stars of the day, and then the Swedish Open, it was a natural progression for Tony to follow me into the England side and we hit it off from the start.

We enjoyed great success playing pairs together, notably on several trips to America. On one occasion over there we were invited to do an exhibition in the Long Bar in a godforsaken cowboy town called Antelope Valley in the middle of the Nevada desert. We were to open up against a couple of the local players, each playing a leg of 1,001. I threw first and hit the sort of form you can only dream about, rattling in a run of 180s in a 19-dart leg. Anyone who knows their darts will tell you how special that is – we rarely play that well in practice, let alone a match situation. The cowboys of Antelope Valley loved it and were whoopin' and hollerin' as they threw their hats up in the air.

'Yee hah Bobby!' they yelled, as they swarmed around me demanding high fives. They'd never seen anything like it and I was their favourite darts player – for all of five minutes.

'Bloody hell, how am I supposed to follow that?' grumbled Tony.

I settled back to relax and watched on as Tony began with two darts into the treble 20 bed. Then, he was distracted by the sight of a fly walking up the wall at the side of the board.

'Anyone got a camera?' he asked. 'Watch me pin that fly to the wall.' With the utmost precision Tony pinned the poor fly with his third dart and the place erupted again. They all went crazy, screaming and shouting as a queue formed to take a photo of the poor insect.

Tony was lifted high on someone's shoulders and paraded around the room to huge applause. Meanwhile, I was left on my own, sitting in a corner reflecting on how quickly life can change. No one cared about my 19-dart leg anymore, just the fly!

A few days later we'd enjoyed some down-time in Las Vegas a little too much. We'd taken quite a lot of refreshment on board and when we walked outside in the midday sun it hit us. It was boiling hot and we were hammered, not a good combination. Somehow, we made it back to our digs, giggling all the way. As we reached our destination Tony rushed forwards and dived head first into the swimming pool, still fully clothed.

I was laughing my head off and did the same but as soon as I hit the water I knew that I was in trouble. Although I was quite a strong swimmer I'd taken a huge gulp of water and was struggling to reach the surface. I was drowning.

Just then Tony grabbed me by the collar and lifted me up. Somehow, he helped me out of the water and even emptied my pockets and dried out all my banknotes whilst I was recovering. We'd both been very stupid and I'd genuinely thought I was going to die.

Later in life Tony used to come round to my place a lot with his youngest and he'd play with our two. He'd had children with his first missus and then had the snip but when he married his new partner Moira, he had it all reversed and they had a boy together, called Jake. When the three boys were playing at ours they'd all get a bit giddy and be dashing about, here, there and everywhere and I'd tick them off. 'Stop running about, calm down – little fuckers.'

They'd carry on, making the dogs bark and all sorts, so I'd be effin' and blindin' at them to pack it in. Tony would be appalled and tell Jake that he mustn't listen to Uncle Bobby's naughty language. He'd say, 'It's not a running day today Jake, it's a walking day!'

Little did Tony and Moira realise but Jake would go into the other room with our boys and yell at the top of his voice, 'Fuck, fuck, c**t, c**t!' Little so and so, he hadn't got that from me! We later learned that he'd always been potty-mouthed with our two but whenever Tony was around he acted like butter wouldn't melt in his mouth.

Another player who is sadly no longer with us is Rab Scott, an Essex boy who used to play for the county when I was captain there. Good enough to compete in the BDO World Championship on two occasions, he was as proud as punch when he was eventually selected to play for England. We travelled together and got rooms next to each other at the hotel.

After checking in I asked him if he would meet me in the bar for a pint but he said he wanted to stay in his room and have a bit more practice ahead of his big day.

I could tell he was a bundle of nerves, understandable really as he was about to be playing for his country for the first time, so I again suggested that a drink or two might relax him.

'No, I just want to get on the board,' he said.

So, I was left on my own to have a couple of drinks and went to bed at 11 or 11.30 maybe. My plans for a quiet night were soon in tatters because as soon as my head hit the pillow I heard, 'thud, thud, thud'.

I wondered what it was at first, then heard it again, 'thud, thud, thud'. Then I twigged, Rab was still throwing darts next door. He'd got one of those fixtures you could get to hang the board on the door of your room.

'Thud, thud, thud'. On it went.

About four o'clock I woke up for a wee and could still hear it, 'thud, thud, thud'. I couldn't believe it, this was ridiculous but I left him to it and quickly went back to sleep, only to wake again about sixish. By eight o'clock I'd had enough and got up and asked him if he was coming down for some breakfast. Then I asked him what he'd been up to all night.

'Practising was going well Bobby,' he started. 'Then it got to a point where I said to myself, right, one 180 and then I'm going to bed. Once I've committed to that I keep going, that's the way I practise. Unfortunately, I didn't hit one!'

So, he'd stayed up all night just trying to hit a 180. He was shattered, having had no kip. You could imagine what I called him. Fortunately, he won his match but it's not the way I'd recommend anyone to prepare for their international debut and despite that win I don't think he ever got picked again.

There is one more loss I would like to mention – that of the lovely Harry Kicks junior in the summer of 2024.

The surname of Kicks is legendary in darts circles, with Harry Kicks senior setting up his dartboard manufacturing business in his garage in east London after the war. Originally the company was just called HA Kicks & Sons but then Harry changed it to Winmau, using the first three letters of his wife's names, Winifred Maud. Winmau boards and other darts equipment have been used worldwide for decades and the company enjoyed sponsorship of the World Masters and other top events for many years.

When Harry senior died in 1984, the company passed down to his five sons, one of whom, Harry junior, I have always been very good friends with. In my first book I wrote about how I'd managed to snaffle away the dartboards from my two *News of the World* grand final wins, even though after doing it in 1979 I was strictly warned not to do it again in 1986. Those two boards are proudly on display in George Hall and are two of the most treasured mementos from my career in darts. In order to preserve them for ever I soaked them in resin for ten years then Harry took them away, rewired them and restored them to their former glory.

Harry, a great engineer, invented the Blade Board, which is one of the most popular boards still in use today. After retiring from the business he taught me how to make boards and we decided to make one together, putting them out there with our initials on them – R and H – and with a crown in between the letters. If asked, we said that it stood for Robert and Harry but it could also have been Royal Highness, for the King of Bling!

They were very popular indeed and Eric used to say that they were the best boards he'd ever played on, rare praise from the great man. In the end it was starting to take over our lives a little bit and had become very time-consuming and neither of us wanted that; we'd just done it for the craic really.

I always enjoyed Harry's company, he was a lovely bloke and we made each other laugh so much, so I was gutted when told that he'd died in the summer of 2024.

MINISTER FOR DARTS

JUST BEFORE this book was published, Marie and I spent a few evenings in front of the television watching the Olympic Games from Paris and couldn't believe what we were seeing; rock climbing and breakdancing being recognised as official sports? What's that all about?

I've always thought it would be nice to see darts in the Olympics one day; it's not much different to archery, is it? To me, there's no question that it should be trialled and would reward all the hours of dedication and practice that the top players put into it.

Anyway, seeing those other 'sports' getting their opportunity brought back memories of the time back in the 1990s that I tried to get darts recognised as an official sport.

You've all heard the arguments over the bar in your local, I assume, between those that play darts and those that don't.

'It's not a sport, it's just a pub game …' they say, and the bickering goes on and on. I decided back then that it was time to put an end to it and give them all a kick up the arse and get it sorted.

I happened to meet up with the MP Bob Russell – now Sir Bob – at some charity events in Colchester and he assured me that he was happy to offer some help once I'd told him what I was trying to do. We discovered that there was a process to follow that would get things moving but we needed to put on a darts demonstration inside the House of Commons. Lots of phone calls were made, we got all sorts of men, ladies and youth team players involved and all were happy to come on board and fight our corner. The prestigious Terrace Marquee was booked to stage the event and we intended to invite as many MPs as we could to come and witness it, so we could try to earn their support.

The only fly in the ointment was that the proposal would need official backing from the governing body, in our case the BDO – and a deposit of £500 would have to be handed over. Wrongly, I assumed this wouldn't be an issue, but when I went to Olly Croft and told him what I was planning to do, he refused to go along with it and felt it was a waste of the organisation's funds. Can you believe it?

I tried, with help from Bob, to get things moving but then everything ground to a halt anyway because Parliament was about to be closed for a period due to refurbishment.

'Fuck it,' I thought and left the matter there, not knowing whether I'd have been wasting my time anyway. But Bob Russell had another go a couple of years later and did eventually manage to get darts acknowledged as a sport by the UK Sports Council. So, next time you hear that argument starting up in your local, you can bring it to a quick resolution – darts IS a sport, thanks to the work put in by Bobby George and his MP, Sir Bob Russell!

I have often wondered if perhaps I should have stood as an MP, because I've always had a little bit of an interest in how the country is being run and I seem to get asked for an opinion, whatever the matter at hand.

Robert Francis George, Minister for Darts and Common Sense, can you imagine it?

As the Legends of the Oche tour proved, it's important that we all rub along together or you can easily spoil a good thing. That, in my humble opinion, is what happened in 2016 when the country was asked to vote in the Brexit referendum. How we got to that stage I'm not sure, but there were clearly elements of society that no longer wanted to carry on as we had been doing: they wanted change. Some of their arguments centred on the belief that they couldn't get jobs in this country and had to go on the drip (the dole) as a result. They claimed that people were coming here through open borders and taking their jobs. Others felt it wrong that the lawmakers in Brussels were having too much say in the way we ran our country and wanted more of a say in things. There were two sides to it, of course.

I'm just a simple darts player but I couldn't understand why people wanted to leave the EU: we'd been in a binding contract for 42 years with them and as far as I was concerned we'd had no aggro. I listened to all of the arguments for and against and was firmly in the Remain camp.

Word must have spread, because someone I'd met briefly a couple of years before got in touch to ask if I'd be interested in doing a short clip for social media to spell out the importance of remaining in the EU. Calum Campbell is the son of Alastair Campbell, best known for the various roles he undertook during Tony Blair's time as prime minister. I'd actually met Alastair in 2005 when he came down to the Lakeside and we'd chatted over a leg of darts.

His son Calum had been in some dark places during a personal battle with alcoholism and ended up living on the streets of London. Through willpower and the help of friends he had turned his life around and was now doing all he could to help others who were also struggling. I was invited to go with him and his mother, Fiona Millar, when they were setting off to feed the homeless one night. Mistakenly, I thought many of them would be refugees who had ended up here and simply had no one to turn to. Sadly, as it transpired, there were lots of ex-servicemen in need of help. Several had lost limbs and couldn't get work, all had fallen on hard times and were homeless. It was desperately sad to witness and hit home how fortunate some of us are not to be in that situation. I admired Calum for what he was doing and told him to call if there was anything I could do to help.

So, when he did ring, sometime later, I thought it would be about one of his charitable undertakings, not anything to do with how I intended to vote on 23 June. Calum asked me what I thought about Brexit and I told him that I didn't want to leave but that was my opinion and I wasn't going to be a spokesman for the Labour party or anything like that.

He assured me that wasn't his intention but asked if I'd do a short video clip for social media for him. I was more than happy to help a mate out and it only took a couple of minutes to come up with an idea.

Wearing a Remain t-shirt, the video showed me hitting a bullseye and then saying into the camera, 'It only takes me five seconds to hit a bullseye and it only takes five seconds to put an X in the box.

'It takes five seconds to stop people fucking up your future … and mine!'

Then I marked a large X on the camera lens and ended with 'Lovely jubbly.'

Obviously once the social media clip had been seen by all and sundry, everyone wanted to get my take on Brexit. One television reporter asked me how bad it would be for the country if we did leave. Answering as honestly as I could, I said, 'I don't know because the ship has never been down that river. We've been going this way for 42 years and never run aground. Mind you, you've got to be a good captain to steer the boat in the right place.' It was all pretty much made-up nonsense because all I really felt like saying was, 'Don't fuck up your life, or mine.'

As we now know, the vote went the other way, people too worried about people coming here from abroad and taking their jobs or going straight on the drip. Anyhow, I had to laugh when a day or two later David Cameron resigned as prime minister and virtually said the same thing in his leaving speech.

One of the more bizarre pieces of television I've been involved in was before the general election in 2019 when the BBC asked me to debate politics, or 'bolloctics' as I call it, with another celebrity but our identities were kept secret from each other until we met, over a coffee.

I was sat there, enjoying my flat white, when in walked – on first sight – a beautiful young lady, dressed in over-the-top thigh-high pink boots and with vivid pink nails and a shock of gorgeous blonde hair. 'Hellooooo,' I said – but I sensed that something dodgy was going on here. Bobby wasn't going to be fooled.

Laughing, I said, 'Can I call you darling?'

My new companion said, 'Oh, yes please.'

I realised it was a geezer, a very good looking one, the Australian drag queen Courtney Act. Real name Shane Jenek, the Aussie star was great fun to have a verbal joust with, although Courtney's get-out was that, as an Australian, she couldn't vote for any of the candidates. We fulfilled our end of the bargain and discussed most of the topics of the day, including Boris and Brexit, before time was called.

We flirted a bit at the end for the cameras. I said to Courtney, 'If you had a pair of tits doll, I'd marry you.'

'Hang on,' she said. 'I'll go and get them, they're in the car!'

There must be something about general elections and getting Bobby George on television because I received a curious request for the night of the 2024 election. I've established a good relationship with GB News and was happy to be part of their 'Election Party', held, curiously enough, at the Circus Tavern in Purfleet and presented by Patrick Christys and Michelle Dewsbury.

Formerly home of the PDC World Championship, the Tavern is a great venue for darts and I'm lucky enough to have played there a few times in local events, exhibitions and, of course, the League of Legends. Never though, did I expect it to be the beating heart of the news channel's election special.

The place was packed, with a combination of friends and family of the channel and members of the general public who'd blagged their way in. Entertainment in the form of a few musical acts came on the main stage, whilst they'd put a dartboard up in one of the bars so that their guests could come and try their luck and have a throw. The trouble was, there was no light above the board. It was completely dark. I was trying to attract some interest, inviting people to come and have a go and see how they would get on. Despite having to show most of them how to stand properly and how to throw accurately, most of them still couldn't hit the board and if they did we couldn't see where it landed. There were plenty of television cameramen in there, so I grabbed one and asked if he could shine a light on the board for half an hour. We all got on a bit better after that but it was one of my more unusual bookings, shall we say.

For most that are involved, election night is a long old slog but I was back home in bed and well out of it before midnight, only hearing the full outcome the next morning.

Whatever your political standpoint, you'll have heard, I'm sure, that both Nigel Farage and Lee Anderson gained seats for the Reform Party. As it happens, I've been on television shows with both of them in recent times and enjoyed chatting to both.

I met Nigel Farage on something called *Talking Pints*, where he interviewed a personality each week over a pint or two. He'd clearly done some homework because he knew all about me and my life and asked how I'd gone from digging tunnels and laying granite floors to suddenly becoming one of the biggest stars in the world of darts.

'How did you do it so quickly?' he asked.

I told him that obviously I had a gift for playing darts and then, tongue-in-cheek, I quipped, 'Everyone has a gift for doing something Nigel, obviously you haven't found yours yet!'

I found him to be very easy to chat to and we got round to the subject of the pub, somewhere that we'd both spent quite a bit of our lives inside by the sound of it. Asking my opinion on the current state of our public houses I told him that things were very different nowadays. Once upon a time you could go into your local pub and it was a bit like flicking through the Yellow Pages. Looking around you could see people from all walks of society: there would be electricians, mechanics, gardeners and greengrocers, everyone and everything all there under one roof. So-and-so over there would be a carpenter, he was a bricklayer, someone else was a vet and everyone knew everyone else. If you needed a hand, someone down the local boozer would be able to help or know someone that could.

Many years ago I was practising on the dartboard in my old local, the King George V in Gants Hill, Ilford. This chap came up to me and said, 'Hi Bob, do you know anyone who wants a couple of weeks' work labouring for me?'

'No idea mate,' I said, looking around. The place was absolutely packed. 'Just ask them.'

He seemed a bit timid and clearly thought he'd be out of his depth if he started shouting out, so I did it for him.

'Quiet everyone,' I bellowed. They all went quiet and looked at me. 'This guy wonders if anyone wants a couple of weeks' work labouring for him.'

There was this bloke called Kissy – I don't know how he got his nickname but everyone knew him as Kissy – he always had a suit on and you'd always find him with a pint in one hand and a betting slip in the other. He never did any actual work, he was always on the ponce – you know, on the dole and always having some little earner on the side.

Kissy put his hand up and everyone remained quiet and looked at him. 'How much are you paying?' he asked.

The bloke said, 'I'll pay you what you're worth.'

Kissy laughed at him and sneered, 'I ain't working for that!' The place erupted.

That was what it was like at the time, they were the characters of the pub and every local had them.

I'm not sure it's like that anymore: you go into a pub now and you don't know anyone. Nobody talks to each other, they just sit in a corner on their own, minding their own business.

Life used to revolve around our public houses and your local was a central part of the community.

It was a form of recreation, down-to-earth people getting through life by chatting to their mates and putting the world to rights. That's how it was, you'd go down to the pub and chat to your mates, perhaps have a game of darts and a few beers. Good times. That's what I discussed with Farage anyway, not deep, meaningful stuff that's going to change the country's outlook, just my thoughts on how things have changed.

Lee Anderson seemed quite a nice bloke when I met him and I warmed to him even more when he told me about his background. You know me, I've always believed in getting up and getting on with it, putting a shift in to earn the 'bees and honey', so I was hugely impressed that he'd actually grafted for a living before turning to politics. He'd been a coalminer for ten years, down that very deep, black hole working alongside his dad. That's a proper hard slog. A politician that had actually done some work in his life – down there on the coal face, quite literally.

HERE'S JOHNNY!

IN THE first book I told of my limited experiences in the movie industry. At the time it just about amounted to one film, a gangster movie called *One Man and His Dog*. Adapted from a screenplay called *Dog*, I played a gangland boss called Tony Barton, who loved his darts, was a right old villain, and was always dripping in gold. (Can you see why I got the part?)

Other offers have poured in, sorry dripped in, as a result. They must have been impressed with my gangster grooves because I had a bit-part in a film called *Gatwick Gangstas*. Once again, my role was short but my impact was pivotal to the plot. A woman and a bloke were playing snooker and I had to walk in with a shotgun and shoot them.

Bang! Bang! Done. Please send Marie the royalties cheque.

I was on more familiar ground in *Poison Arrows*, a darts-themed extravaganza released in 2022, as Ray Stubbs and I were asked to play ourselves. Another darts-related film I appeared in was called *Broken Arrow*, which was about a one-armed darts player who competes in the qualifying rounds to play darts in the Paralympics. I only had a few lines in it but was more than happy to help out in a cast that also included *The Royle Family*'s Sue Johnston and Chris Simmons from *The Bill*.

Everything I've done I've thoroughly enjoyed and it has always whetted my appetite to do more, so I was unlikely to turn down the opportunity to expand my repertoire of skills when I received an invitation to be a consultant on a film called *London Fields*. It followed on from the successful book of the same name, written by Martin Amis, which centred upon Keith Deller's World Championship victory in 1983, although with different fictional characters.

Initially, my contributions extended only to an advisory role, letting the film directors and producers into all the little secrets that go into the preparation and execution of a World Championship final. Lest you forget, I have played in two of them! My years of presenting on television also came in handy, as I explained the benefits of split screen coverage; the image of the board on one side of your screen and the player on the other. The more I told them, the more they wanted to know and then some bright spark had the idea that I should be written into the film, playing the role of the MC. Suddenly things got a bit more interesting and I admit, I even asked Marie who I should thank in my acceptance speech on Oscars night!

There certainly seemed to be a large enough budget to have dreams about this becoming a Hollywood blockbuster. I was told I'd be picked up and chauffeur-driven from my home into the studios, near the O2 in east London. What they didn't say was that my ride would be in a Bentley and that it would be top-of-the-range luxury all the way. It was drizzling with rain when we arrived outside the venue but studio staff came straight up to the car and had umbrellas ready to hold over Marie and myself.

Then I heard some comments coming my way. 'Bloody hell, is that your car, Bobby?' It was Peter Manley, three-time world finalist. 'One Dart,' as he's known, had been brought out to work as an extra on the film, alongside a few London-based players. Andy Fordham, Scott Mitchell, Steve West and Richie Howson were also there, all huddled together under a canvas to keep out of the rain.

'No, they picked me up in that,' I said, grinning towards them all.

'What, you come by chauffeured car, and we had to come by fucking underground?' was the expected reaction.

I just laughed, more so when someone announced, 'Your trailer is ready, Mr George.' There were certainly some green-eyed monsters amongst my darting buddies as we were led to our trailer and brought some breakfast.

Filming took place in a warehouse, close to the O2. They must have spent thousands and thousands on the set, making it look exactly like it did on Embassy finals night. Amongst the star-studded cast were Billy Bob Thornton, Jim Sturgess, Jason Isaacs, Theo James, Lily Cole, Cara Delevingne and Amber Heard, although Jim was the only one I had spent any time with because he had been over to George Hall and got all the info.

I ran through some of my lines and gave an opinion or two on what they were planning for the darts scenes and was looking forward to doing a few more scenes when they called time on the day. We were meant to go back and do some more filming over the next few days but I received a message to say that they needed to take a break as one of the actors had pulled out and a replacement needed to be found.

I wondered if it was just a way of letting me down gently and that would be the last I'd hear from them. Marie was more positive though, and felt it was just a normal thing that was likely to happen on film sets. She even speculated that they might get Johnny Depp in as a short-notice replacement, as he was with Amber Heard at the time. The name was familiar to me but that was about all. I was aware of the *Pirates of the Caribbean* films but hadn't seen them and didn't know anything else about the bloke.

The call to resume filming came a few days later and back we went, after again being chauffeured in. I wandered around saying hello to everybody again and was stood on the stage when a chap sidled up to me and said, 'Alright Bob?'

I said, 'Yes, thanks mate,' not knowing who he was but generally just being polite.

He asked if I wanted a smoke but I quickly remembered them being a bit arsey about where we could and couldn't smoke, so I told him it wasn't allowed.

'Fuck 'em,' said the stranger. 'I'll smoke where I want.' Then he lit up a Golden Virginia roll-up.

Passing time, I asked him what he was doing there today.

'Got to do a bit,' he replied, in a twang that wasn't too dissimilar from where I'd grown up.

'Oh yeah,' I said, 'what part of London are you from?'

He seemed to be taken aback. 'Not from London, I'm a Yank,' he explained.

I thought he sounded just like a Cockney and told him so. 'Fuck me, you'd make a good spy,' I said, and we both laughed. 'I'd have sworn you come from London, you talk just like me,' I told him.

'No,' said my new friend. 'I'm doing an English part, a Cockney part, so I've got to talk like that.' He told me to hang on while he fetched his script and came back with a curious expression on his face. 'One of my lines is, "Do you think I'm a c**t?"

I laughed at the words he'd been given but he thought I was laughing at him. 'How would you say it, then?' he queried.

Looking at his lines and the context it was being said in, I told him, 'If it was me I'd probably say "Do you think I'm some sort of c**t or what?"

He lapped it up and couldn't write it down quickly enough. I could see he was scribbling out the original words and then began walking around the stage practising: 'Do you think I'm some sort ...'

I noticed Marie giving me daggers from the side of the stage. 'What's the matter?' I asked her.

'Aren't you going to introduce me to your friend?' she whispered, clearly excited about something.

'Why, who is it?' I innocently queried.

When she told me that it was Johnny Depp I was taken aback; I genuinely had no idea who I'd been speaking to. Just then he came back towards us and Marie wasted no time in making her own introductions.

'Hello Johnny, I'm Bobby's wife,' she announced, shaking his hand.

'I feel like I've known your husband for years,' he told her.

The rest of the day was taken up with filming, really intense stuff and the reality was uncanny. One of the actors, Jim Sturgess, was playing a character that was based on me. He did his walk-on with the cloak, the gold rings and everything. Peter Manley groaned when he saw him: 'What the fuck is this?' he sighed. 'The Bobby George story?'

Depp was also a darts player in the film and there was a bit where he was being asked by an interviewer if he was going to win. The script had his lines as, 'Yes, I win everything,' but I told him to say, instead, 'Course I'm going to win, it's Christmas every day for me, innit?'

They changed the script and put my words in. I thought 'Fucking hell, I'm a Hollywood scriptwriter now!'

There was another section where Depp's character approached the female lead and started to kiss her passionately. As MC I had to lean towards the caller at that point and say, 'Look at that, he's got his tongue right down her neck ain't he … I thought he'd come here for a darts match, not a blue movie.'

Amber Heard was the female lead, of course, as well as being Johnny's real-life girlfriend at the time. She got her kiss and before we left them Marie got a kiss from the great man as well.

It was great to be involved in something like that and made even better by getting to spend a bit of time with such a renowned actor as Johnny Depp. He told me that he was thinking of buying a property in London and had earmarked a flat that might be suitable in Belgravia for a knock-down £5 million.

'It's a shithole, mate,' I told him. 'There'll be no garden or fuck all there and you'll never find anywhere to park. It'll just be a flat roof looking at all the shitty buildings.'

I don't know if he thought I was joking or not. I wasn't!

How Johnny took the Cockney accent off so well was a real surprise to me, although it was immediately apparent what a brilliant actor he is. In between takes he told me all about his childhood, growing up in Kentucky and about the Native American genes on his mother's side of the family.

The only disappointment about the whole thing was that the film ended up in all sorts of legal disputes, with lawsuits flying here, there and everywhere amongst the producers and director. When it was eventually released in the United States it got nothing more than a lukewarm reception.

My Oscars speech will have to wait for another day!

REDDRAGON
AIRFLOW
STEALTH

The King of Bling on his throne at Ardleigh village fete

Cocktoe anyone?

Legends of the Oche, with Eric and Lowey

Reverend Bobby, on Don't Tell The Bride

Showbiz Darts, with James Hewitt, Michael Le Vell, Holly Willoughby and Phil Tufnell

Brian McFadden kipped on our sofa in Who's Doing The Dishes?

Engelbert tried all night but couldn't win a leg on his visit to George Hall

Laughs aplenty with Jim Davidson on A Leg with Bobby

With Johnny Depp on the set of our movie

With some more of my mates
... Dennis Priestley

Peter Manley

Luke Humphries

Fun is always guaranteed with… Michael van Gerwen and Jonny Clayton

A master of his craft, I've worked alongside Ray Stubbs since 1980

Gone To Pot: American Road Trip: *We opted for the family-sized pack (above)*

With executive producer Kevin Mundye

Marie meets my fellow travellers

The Real Marigold Hotel *cast. Me (far left), then Sylvester McCoy, Wayne Sleep, Patti Boulaye, Jan Leeming, Roy Walker, Miriam Margolyes and Rosemary Shrager.*

I had a natty little suit made in India but it's too hot to wear at exhibitions!

The George Family

BOBBY THE PUNDIT

I USED to love working for the BBC at the Lakeside World Championships – it gave me an opportunity to stay in touch with the current crop of players as well as broadening my experience of working in live television.

It all started in 1998 when I'd failed to qualify for the Worlds and I was asked if I'd be a studio guest for the event. There was always lots for me to learn but I made sure I did my homework on all of the players and treated them with the respect I'd expect to get.

The BBC must have been pleased with what I had to offer because I kept being invited back and those couple of weeks in January became as important to me as when I'd been playing in the event.

Whilst you can never claim to know everything about a subject, there wasn't much I hadn't encountered during my time as one of the game's top professionals and I think I'd earned the right to have my opinions respected.

Over all the years that I worked on the event, I was able to share a microphone with most of the game's top broadcasters, starting with Peter Purves, then the likes of David Icke, Dougie

Donnelly, Clare Balding, Colin Murray and Ray Stubbs as the lead presenters.

On the darts side of things Olly Croft, the founder of the BDO and long-serving tournament director, always kept a firm hand on the tiller but there were others who had a big say in how the event ran. None more so than the late Peter Dyke. During the many years of Embassy sponsorship, Peter was head of special promotions for Imperial Tobacco and not only ran the darts for them but also their other high-profile events, like the World Snooker Championship, the universities' Boat Race and the televised fishing tournaments.

Peter was alright, a bit funny and a bit rude and a bit of a posh Cockney like me! We rubbed along alright and he even came and had some corporate days at my fishing lakes. The thing about him though, was that he didn't like kids. One year they had a do after the Lakeside final and everyone was invited except for the kids: they didn't want the little ones in there. Fair enough, if that's what you want to do but mine had been there all week with Marie and I wasn't going to go without them.

Peter's deputy was a nice fella called John Exon, who took the time to thank me for everything and said he'd see me at the do later. I told him that I wouldn't be going because I'd said I wouldn't go without the kids.

'Oh, don't worry about that,' he said, and handed over some tickets for myself and the family.

It didn't take long for Dyke to spot us and he came straight over and had a quiet word. 'Glad you've come Bobby, but how did you get tickets for the children?'

'John gave them to me,' I replied.

'Fucking hell,' he mumbled. 'That bloke would invite the entire audience if he could!'

Ray Stubbs is the one I've known and worked with for the longest – we first met at the Unipart British Masters in the 1980s and have remained in touch ever since. He once accompanied me with a film crew on a trip to Germany to entertain the troops and it was shown on *Sportsnight* after my 1994 world final.

You can't beat being on live television for giving you a certain sort of adrenalin. It's all fly-by-the-seat-of-your-pants stuff: one take, no mistakes broadcasting. If you say something then it's out there, no going back and doing an edit. In that sort of environment, you always need to be able to rely on your partner and know that if the chips are down he can pull you through. Working with Ray for all these years I've never failed to appreciate his professionalism and know that he's always sharp enough to assess a situation and leap in and take over if an interview isn't going as planned.

Mind you, on one occasion I had to think on my feet after Ray had blurted out the wrong name. The start of one evening session had Ted Hankey down to play in the first match so, as is customary, we deemed it appropriate that I talk about him for a couple of minutes. Well, what can you say? You can't talk for five seconds about Ted Hankey, let alone two minutes. There's the Count stuff and his bats but that's about it. Anyway, I was going over a few thoughts and was ready to go as soon as I got my cue from Ray.

There were all sorts of noises going off in my ears. It's an extraordinary experience in the few moments before you go on air; there are lots of different voices in our earpieces. The one to listen out for is that of the director; what he says goes.

Then the countdown started in our ears, to tell us that we were going out live on air … 10, 9, 8, 7, 6, 5 …

Ray did his introduction piece and then said, out of nowhere:

'Well Bob, what do you think of Andy Fordham?'

Talk about asking me to think on my feet, I'm full of Hankey thoughts and all ready to go to town on what I can say about him; now I'm being asked about someone else. I blurted stuff about Fordham being a bit of a cartoon character and suiting his Viking personality and all that stuff. His tattoos, his arms that are bigger than most people's entire body and other nonsense just to get through the piece.

I was getting there, and then I heard the voice of the director in my ear. 'Well done Bobby, tell Ray he's a c**t.'

None of the audience could hear that, of course. But Ray and myself clearly did and we were both dying to laugh, although Ray was now looking at me and wondering if I was about to call him the most unforgiveable word on live television.

That was certainly a moment that neither of us had bargained for; another was when I was asked to go and do a live interview on my own for the BBC. It took place in the canteen at Bridlington after Michael van Gerwen had beaten Martin Adams in the final of the World Masters. He was obviously high with his success and I tried to tap into that.

'Did that feel good, Michael?' was my opener.

‘Yes, very guds,’ replied the Dutchman.

‘Did you find it difficult at all, because you were behind in sets but then fought back and he missed a double to let you in?’ was my follow-up.

Michael came back with, ‘I thought to myself “this is going to be a fucking hard game”.’

I nearly died but managed to apologise to the viewers and gently tell MVG that we were on live television and he couldn’t use that word. His answer had an element of truth in it, ‘Why not? Everyone in England uses it all the time.’

Oh boy, thank you Michael, I thought and moved on quickly.

Thankfully, moments like that are few and far between …

SI SI SENIOR

IN RECENT times I've been privileged to be part of the team that covers the seniors' events on television. Once again working alongside Ray Stubbs, I've enjoyed the uncertainty of going to each event and having no idea who might come out on top.

It has become hugely popular very quickly and the standard is rising with every tournament. In many ways it's a little bit like old-fashioned darts – or like it used to be in my day. The crowd are respectful and appreciate what they're watching and many of those that come along have got a darts background that involves the phrase 'best of order, game on', and they give the players their utmost respect.

Everyone is polite and there's no nastiness involved and it's really interesting to see how the players perform. Some stopped playing top-level darts and have had their faith in the game restored by having the chance to play against some of their old contemporaries once again. Others might not have made it first time around and are now reaping the benefit from a lifetime of playing good standard darts. Richie Howson is one who didn't have that big breakthrough on either the BDO or PDC tours yet is a regular challenger for the senior titles.

Although I was concentrating mainly on my exhibition work when I hit 50, I think I might have been tempted to play had the seniors' tour been around at that time. All the events are great fun and if darts is in your blood then why stop just because you've reached a certain age? You can hear a pin drop at times when you're watching some of the tightest contests and the support for the individual players is wonderful to see. Darts has always been excellent, with the players willing to give a little bit back to the fans and at these events they all come out and mix with the audience whether they've won or lost. They've all been around long enough to know the value of keeping the fans loyal. Many of those supporters have been there for us for years, decades even, and it's not asking too much for the players to give up a couple of minutes to sign a few autographs and stand for a couple of selfies.

The events have become hugely popular and it's staggering to see the number of people who are prepared to travel huge distances to attend. There's always a large contingent who come over from Belgium and Holland to back their favourites. At the Circus Tavern in recent years we've even had visits from several members of the Mongolian Darts Organisation. They come along and dress up and enjoy themselves.

I'm not sure if my knowledge of that fine country is anything near to the truth but I was talking to one of them and he told me he'd won their national championship. For a laugh, I asked him what he'd got for winning. 'Was it a horse?' I enquired. Imagine my surprise when he said, 'Yes – and the runner-up got a goat!'

My knowledge of Mongolia actually only extends to watching a documentary about Attila the Hun. What a bastard he was, marching off to invade neighbouring countries and slaughtering two million people. He didn't care who or what got in his way, soldiers, civilians, horses, anything.

Remind you of anyone? Did I tell you I saw Putin when I was in St Petersburg?

'Alright Bob, what are you doing here?'

'Just come to look and see if this is a nice place to retire, Vladimir my old mate!'

THE GAME IS IN GOOD HANDS

TWO OF my dearest darts friends are Colin Lloyd and Wayne Mardle, who I see regularly and often go out and about to exhibitions with. In his prime, 'Jaws' Lloyd was good enough to win two of the PDC's premier events, the World Matchplay and the World Grand Prix. He often used to come to mine and we'd practise together but I had to push him, make him hit 64 double 16s before he could knock off. That's not as easy as it perhaps sounds: you've got to focus and maintain your concentration for a lengthy period, as you would up on the stage.

Eventually, with a cry of relief, he completed the task. 'Good, can I go home now?' he wailed.

'Not yet,' I answered. 'You've got to hit three bullseyes first.' He was mustard at that and sank three into the middle without batting an eyelid. Now he's past his own 'bullseye birthday' I keep telling him to join the seniors' tour and give that a crack. He's easily good enough to scoop up some of the winners' prize money on that tour and apart from being a good craic, it wouldn't take up too much of his time.

Mr Mardle is now well-known to the younger generation as an outstanding commentator and pundit on Sky's television coverage but he was also a hugely talented player, who will probably be the first to admit that he didn't make the most of his ability. He didn't quite achieve the same sort of walk-on status as the King of Bling either but he gave it a good shot, all with a bit of help from yours truly.

In the 2001 Embassy World Championships Wayne reached the semi-finals and he'd started wearing bright Hawaiian shirts for his matches, whilst they introduced the theme song from the US cop show *Hawaii 5-0* as his walk-on music. It was hugely popular and went down a treat with the fans but I didn't think his nickname was right. He was called the 'Mouth of the South' back then. Now I know that fits him like a glove because he can be a gobby so-and-so, but it didn't feel right, with all the Hawaii stuff going on. So, during an interview that year I just said to him, 'Why don't you put a 1 at the end of the Hawaii 5-0, then you'll be Hawaii 501?' I should have charged him for the idea!

Michael van Gerwen is a player that I've known since he was bursting into the ranks as an outstanding teenager and we are often at the same exhibitions. He's great fun to be around and he's always trying to wind me up, calling me grandad or old man. I have to be careful not to leave my darts unattended because he'll either pinch them or steal my flights and pop some of his old ones in them. He gets me in trouble with Marie as well. She's not keen on me smoking but I'll have the odd one now and again. Michael will ask me to pop outside with him at an event and he'll light one up for us both. If I get distracted and talk to someone or stand there signing a couple of autographs, he'll video me with the cigarette then go back inside and show Marie. He's a bad man but I like his company very much and get my own back by calling him a German.

He always bites: 'I'm Dutch Bobby, Dutch – not German.'

I love spending time with Michael: Boy Wonder I call him, although he called himself something different when he put his number into my mobile phone directory. I watched him punch the numbers in but when I went to call him a few days later I couldn't find anything under M or V or G … Eventually he rang me instead and it came up as Best in the World, the cheeky so and so!

His big chum and compatriot Raymond van Barneveld is a similar character in the practice area and also likes to tease me. If I call him German, he always responds with '*Jawohl*.' Both Raymond and Michael are really good lads and I always enjoy working with them both.

I've done a few exhibitions over the last couple of years with Luke Humphries and was delighted for him when he became World Champion. He's worked hard on his fitness, dedicated himself to the sport and deserves all the success that is now coming his way. It's a great story. Wherever he plays, he's usually got his dad sat on the side cheering him on.

Luke has many years at the top of the game ahead of him but he will be well aware that Luke Littler will be there challenging him for all of that time.

Littler brought a new army of followers to the sport by bursting on to the scene at just 16 years of age with a run to the 2024 world final.

Alongside the two Lukes, there are more and more talented youngsters coming through, eager to make their mark in the world of darts and claim a share of the 'bees and honey'. I have done a few exhibition nights with some of the best around and love spending time with them: Gerwyn Price is a good lad, with a physique nearly as good as mine. His Welsh team-mate Jonny Clayton is a lovely guy as well.

It's still great to be involved with them and all of the current stars of the sport and I'm delighted to still be a regular on all the big shows put on by Jason Thame of MODUS and Matt Ward of MDA events. The crowd still love to see my original walk-on in all its glory, with the candelabra and cape. These events attract massive numbers and it's a pleasure to be involved with them and meet all the fans at the VIP meet-and-greets beforehand.

Most of the lads and lasses who play nowadays are really decent people, I can't say a bad word about any of them and I've certainly no ill feeling or jealousy about the money they're on. People are always asking if I'd still like to be playing competitively and I have to say that I would but only because it would mean I was a lot younger. You can't turn the clock back, it would have been great to have been playing for bigger prize money, but I'm proud of my career and glad to have played and done what I did, when I did it.

These days I always tell the lads and lasses to never forget where you come from and if someone asks you for a photograph or an autograph just do it. These people make you and they don't forget if you say no. It takes no more than 30 seconds of your time and people will always remember you for that.

Darts is in a great place right now and I wish all the players the very best in their endeavours. Most of the time I'll make a point of watching the televised events and seeing how they all get on. I prefer the knockouts to the Premier League, where it's the same show week after week and doesn't always grab my attention. Maybe it's a sign that I'm getting a little bit older, that I've lost my enthusiasm for it, for there are plenty of others that do love it and I can't blame them. The events always sell out and there's lots of prize money sloshing about, so everyone is happy to be involved.

These days I'm paid to keep an eye on the seniors' tour and give my thoughts on their tournaments and it's something that I really enjoy. Lovely jubbly!

IN THE MONEY

THE OLDER I get, the more I appreciate family life and I love nothing more than catching up with my brother and sister. We didn't keep in touch for quite a long time in our lives but it's nice to spend some quality time with each other. As kids, Kevin and I used to go fishing quite a lot and it's still something we both enjoy doing when we can, and we've also got away on holiday together.

Heather has worked for a funeral director for many years and shows no signs of slowing up. Along with her brothers, she's never been afraid of rolling up her sleeves and working hard. It's a common trait that we share and whilst we've all had about 80 journeys around the sun we're all still grateful to be doing what we do and for the bonds that we share.

Marie and I treasure our time with them and with the younger members of the family. I'd had children with my first wife Betty and became a grandad to Nicola and Shane's children, Charlie, Daisy and Archie, although we are seldom in touch.

But with my and Marie's two boys, it was a neck-and-neck race as to who would become a dad first, with grandsons Bo and Edward arriving just 23 hours apart. It meant we only had to go to hospital once, so at least I saved on some petrol money! Robert and his wife, Devon, now have two children, Bo and Annalisa, along with Devon's other daughter Summur, whilst Richard has three of his own, Edward, Jesse James and Aida, plus Edward and Aida's half-sister Juno, who completes our set of grandchildren.

What a world they've been born into. How much any of them remember of the pandemic remains to be seen but wasn't it an extraordinary time in our lives? Along with everyone else, I can't believe we were all part of a generation that had to experience nationwide lockdowns due to a deadly virus. Those things only happen in films and the minds of science fiction writers. Yet there we were, back in 2020, locked down, locked in, locked up. At least the weather was nice, eh?

I caught COVID a couple of times, certainly not as bad as some folk got it and I'm not sure how really, as Marie and I kept ourselves to ourselves, but at least being locked down meant I could crack on with a few jobs that needed doing. I'm fortunate that I enjoy being busy and had so much to occupy myself with around the place: cutting down trees, cleaning the lakes and a bit of general ground maintenance. I love doing all that sort of stuff and with the constant bright sunshine that we experienced, I was in my own little utopia.

It didn't need a genius to work out that not everyone was living their best life during those troubled times, because we started to get lots of messages from people who wanted me to send a 'get well soon' or 'missing you' message to one of their friends or loved ones. Five or six companies were picking up on this as well, asking celebrities to send out video messages to people. I was asked if I'd do some and before long it was getting ridiculous, with a dozen or so requests a day to send out something: 'happy birthday', 'happy anniversary', 'keep your pecker up', or whatever. They were tough times for everybody and if getting a word or two from Bobby cheered people up then I was only too happy to help, provided that Marie sorted it all out!

It was lovely to hear some positive feedback from it as well, because we all love a cheery message, don't we? Especially on our birthday, which in my case falls on 16 December.

Last year the grandkids were at the house and everyone was making a fuss of me, whilst Marie was upstairs doing something or other. She'd placed all my cards in a neat pile together and granddaughter Aida kept bringing them to me, one by one, to open. It's nice to open your cards and read a lovely message but after a while ... well, you know. Anyway, she kept bringing the cards and after a dozen or so from family and friends, I tore one open and a tenner popped out.

'Oooh, lovely,' I thought. 'I never get cash in my cards.' Then the same happened again and again and again. Occasionally there would be a £20 note in there as well. This was going nicely: I wasn't reading the cards, just ripping them open as Aida passed them over, and happily stacking up my pile of cash on the arm of the chair.

Admittedly, I was beginning to think that there were more cards than usual and how strange it was for so many to contain money but, you know, people are lovely, so I kept on opening them. Then Marie walked into the room and I heard a scream and then the explosion came. The first lot of cards were my birthday ones but then Aida, in total ignorance, had been handing me envelopes from a pile that contained Christmas cards for family and friends, each with money inside. Marie had spent much of the previous afternoon writing them all out and now had the prospect of having to do them all over again.

'But how was I supposed to know?' I offered, playing dumb and hoping that it would blow over quickly, whilst not wanting to get Aida in trouble either.

'Don't you have eyes?' said my unhappy wife. 'These have all got snowmen, robins and Santa Claus on the front and inside they say Happy Christmas!'

Apparently, according to her, I get dafter as I get older but I don't see that as a bad thing at all, do you? It may be a reason, though, why people are always asking me how I am.

'How are you, Bobby?' or 'How are you doing?' I get it every day and the answer is always the same: 'Still here!'

POSTSCRIPT

I'D JUST like to end the book by saying a fond farewell to all the many wonderful people who have either befriended me or made my time in darts all the more enjoyable. I hope they all rest in peace, and my sincere apologies to anyone I've missed in error:

Billy Lennard, Alan Evans, Nicky Virachkul, Dave Clarke, Jim Sweeney, Leighton Rees, Lorna Croft, Tom Fleetwood, Jack Price, Peter Dyke, Lou Shannon, Lil Coombes, Dot Glidle, Mick Coonan, Della Fleetwood, Mick Getty, Pauline Stafford, Mick Banyard, Jocky Wilson, Sid Waddell, Phill Nixon, John Inniss, Vi Alderman, Freddie Williams, Ken Glidle, Dave Vincent, Martin Fitzmaurice, Dave Lanning, Julie Vickers, Stacey Bromberg, Rick Ney, Alan Robson, Tony Sontag, Eric Bristow, Jim Bowen, Phil Jones, John Cosnett, Gerry Hayward, Olly Croft, Billy Skipsey, Mick Miller, Glen Lazaro, Johnny Brittain, Sheila Busby, Alan Glazier, Ceri Morgan, Dave Kelly, Sam Hawkins, Bruce Spendley, Terry O'Dea, Carl Anderson, Andy Fordham, Rab Scott, Roly Bright, Tony Brown, John Gwynne, Mike Gregory, Dave Swindells, Andy Green, Bob Potter, Pat Williams, Tony Green, Harry Kicks.

And finally, I must mention and thank my old mate Lance Hardy, who was a great family friend and helped me write *Bobby Dazzler* all those years ago. Taken far too soon, Lance's next project was going to be about the life story of Jocky Wilson. I wish they'd both still been around to complete it.

ACKNOWLEDGEMENTS

THANK YOU if you've managed to make it through this far and I hope you've enjoyed getting to know me a little bit better. Putting a book together is quite an eye-opening experience and it certainly wouldn't have happened but for the amazing contributions from so many people.

Almost on a daily basis I'm reminded of various episodes that have occurred over the years, so I owe a debt of gratitude to everyone that has inadvertently jogged my memory about this or that adventure.

I will always be extremely grateful to the entire darting fraternity for being so welcoming whenever I've been around. Fellow players, officials and supporters have always been there for me and whilst we may have uttered the odd cross word to each other over the years, nothing has been left unresolved for long.

Right back to the early days of Paul Durrant – and Team Durro – I've always been looked after by the best sponsors around and can't imagine having had the same career without the backing of Courage Breweries and Winmau.

Nowadays many of my appearances are on the big darts shows put on by MODUS and MDA events, so huge thanks to Jason Thame, Matt Ward and their teams for keeping my diary full.

When I first started playing county darts for Essex, one of the leading officials was Derek Ransom and he called the Essex Masters final that I won in 1976. He told me afterwards that I would go on and win a major tournament but he sadly died soon afterwards. I've never forgotten him and since then I've worked with many other brilliant MCs over the years – and continue to do so – Chubby Brown, Martin Fitzmaurice, Phil Jones, Paul Wilson, Paul Starr, Bruce Spendley, George Noble, Paul Taylor, Roly Bright, John McDonald, Paul Hinks and many others have all been a joy to share a stage with. But I must thank, in particular, two guys who have travelled the length and breadth of the country with me and been at my side for more shows than any of us would care to remember: Little Richard Ashdown and Paul Booth – hopefully you both know how much you mean to me.

Likewise, since giving up competitive darts and spending a lot of time talking about it on television I've been fortunate to work with some of the best broadcasters and presenters around, especially my old mates Ray Stubbs and Colin Murray. To them all, either in front of or behind the camera, your expertise and professionalism has been appreciated. I'd also like to pass on my thanks to Mike Walters for approving the use of an extract from his *Daily Mirror* article on Richie's appearance at Lakeside.

A phone call from Ros Edwards wondering if I'd be free to travel the globe, all in the name of making television programmes, set me on the way to many of the incredible encounters I've relayed in this book, so a huge thanks to her and to all my travel companions on *The Real Marigold Hotel* series and on *Gone To Pot. American Road Trip*.

I must give a big thank you to the fabulous team at Pitch Publishing, especially Jane Camillin, Dean Rockett, Graham Hales and Duncan Olner for their help with this project, to Katie Field for her diligent editing and to Dave Bracegirdle for agreeing to help deliver my stories to a wider audience. I've known Dave for more than 40 years and we were sipping a fruit juice at a seniors' event together when I was told that there were no more copies left in print of my first book.

'Let's do another one!' he said – and we did!

Finally, a big thank you to all my wonderful family, especially Marie. I told her on the day that I met her that we were going to get married and we did. It was the best decision I ever made and there isn't a day that goes by without me appreciating her more and more. Apart from everything else she does to enrich my life, she has worked tirelessly with Dave to help put this book together. Marie – I love you!

So that's it folks, I may be gone tomorrow but right now I'm *Still Here*. I didn't have enough pages to write about all the vaginas I've ever met, so I'm saving that for the next book!

Bobby

PHOTO CREDITS

Front cover: Duncan Olner

Photo Block A

All the photographs have been supplied from Bobby and Marie George's private collection, except where indicated. Every effort has been made to seek permission of the rights holder.

Page 1 – Paul Booth's private collection,photographer Mick Ellison

Page 7 – top, from Paul Booth's private collection

Page 8 – top, from Paul Booth's private collection, photographer Mick Ellison

Photo Block B

Page 5 Peter Manley photograph, from Paul Booth's private collection

Pages 6 Jonny Clayton photograph from Dave Bracegirdle's private collection

Page 7 *Gone To Pot* photographs supplied by Kevin Mundye

Page 8 *Marigold* photographs supplied by Ros Edwards

Back cover: supplied by Ros Edwards

INDEX